The Formation of Christian Europe

An Illustrated History of the Church

Created and Produced by Jaca Book

An outline by chapter can be found on the last two pages of this volume.

The Formation of Christian Europe

An Illustrated History of the Church

From 600 to 900

Translated and adapted by John Drury
Illustrated by Franco Vignazia

 Winston Press   430 Oak Grove   Minneapolis, Minnesota 55403

Published in Italy under the title
La via dei barbari: La chiesa e la sua storia
Copyright © 1979, Jaca Book Edizioni

**Licensed publisher and distributor
of the English-language edition:**

Winston Press, Inc.
430 Oak Grove
Minneapolis, Minnesota 55403
United States of America

Agents:
Canada—
    LeDroit/Novalis-Select
    135 Nelson St.
    Ottawa, Ontario
    Canada   KIN   7R4

Australia, New Zealand, New Guinea, Fiji Islands—
    Dove Communications, Pty. Ltd.
    203 Darling Road
    East Malvern, Victoria   3145
    Australia

United Kingdom, Ireland, and South Africa—
    Fowler-Wright Books, Ltd.
    Burgess St.
    Leominster, Herefordshire
    England

Created and produced by Jaca Book, Milan
Color selection: Carlo Scotti, Milan
Printing: Grafiche Lithos Carugate, Milan
Binding: LEM Opera, Milan

History Consultant: The Rev. Marvin R. O'Connell
                Professor of History, University of Notre Dame

Winston Staff: Mark Brokering, Florence Flugaur—editorial
                Chris Larson, Keith McCormick—design

Library of Congress Catalog Card Number: 79-67833
ISBN: 0-03-056827-7

5 4 3 2 1

Slavs
Huns
Goths
Ostrogoths
Visigoths
Lombards
Vandals
Franks
Burgundians
Angles

Saxons
Basques
Arabs

seemed as if the world were falling apart. Yet, at the same time, new and powerful forces were at work developing a new culture. In Arabia, a religion called Islam came into being. It grew very strong and helped form a new civilization in parts of the Middle East, Asia, Africa, and even Spain. In Rome, the popes established closer ties between the Church and the powerful Franks. Missionaries were sent to spread Christ's Gospel to the western lands. These were the first steps that would lead to the formation of the group of nations we know as Europe.

The map on these pages shows part of the large mass of land that today we know as Europe, Asia, and Africa. The arrows show the paths of the tribal migrations. Europe is the northwestern section of the map. It is interesting to compare this map with one in a modern atlas that shows the names and boundaries of today's countries. These boundaries do not appear on the map in this book, because these countries had not been established back in the year 600. But in this book, we will often refer to these regions using the modern names, such as Germany, France, and Italy.

ruled by Rome. These people were barbarians, and they did not have the learning and laws that were part of Roman life. Under barbarian rule, the quality of life became poorer.

The emperor Justinian, who ruled in Constantinople from 527-565, tried, but failed, to regain control of northern Africa and Italy. He also tried to improve government by collecting and organizing the Roman laws. Today, Justinian is remembered mainly for his collection of Roman laws, known as Justinian's Code.

To many people living then, it must have

2. The Lombard people crossed the Alps in the year 568 and moved southward into Italy. There they took control over many sections of northern Italy.

The Lombards, a Germanic people, came from lands north and east of Italy. Other tribes there had threatened the Lombards, and they wanted to move farther south to escape their enemies. Their chance came in 550, when they were hired by the Byzantine emperor, Justinian, to fight in his war against the Ostrogoths, who had taken over Italy.

Justinian won the war, and after the Ostrogoths were defeated, the Lombards

decided to move into Italy. They knew that the Byzantine empire was worn out from the long war and would not be able to send an army to fight them off. They knew, too, that the cities of Italy were not strong enough to fight off an invasion.

So the Lombards crossed the Alps in 568 and spread throughout northern Italy. Although the Byzantine emperor kept control of the important city of Ravenna, the Lombards took over many sections of the Italian peninsula, even in the south, without much difficulty.

The Lombards were not just raiders. They were a whole society of people of all ages on the move—children, women, and men. They were well-organized, able fighters. Their king, Alboin, led them, aided by the dukes he had chosen from among his chieftains. These dukes commanded the military divisions, and they ruled sections of territory called duchies.

A number of Lombard duchies were set up in northern Italy, among them Cividale and Spoleto. The city of Pavia in the valley of the Po River fought off the Lombards for three years, but they finally gave up. Pavia became the capital city of the Lombard king.

For the next hundred years, three different important centers of power existed in Italy: Pavia, the capital of the Lombards and the most powerful of the three; Ravenna, the city controlled by the Byzantine emperor and protected by his navy; and Rome, the city of the pope.

When the Lombards settled in Italy, their way of life began to change. The Lombard dukes began to pay more attention to their own lands, and their feelings of unity with the king grew less strong. After their years of wandering, the Lombards enjoyed this more comfortable life as rulers of people who tilled the fields.

The people of Italy, however, hated the Lombards for a long time because the Lombards were a crude people who had invaded their land. Besides this, the people of Italy were Catholic Christians, while some of the Lombards were pagans and the rest were followers of the Arian form of Christianity.

3. The Lombards brought more unity and security to the land they had conquered. Slowly, they were accepted by some of the natives.

The invading Lombards were hated at first by the Italians. As the years passed, however, the Italians began to see that some good things had happened because of the Lombards. The most important thing was that the Lombards protected them from other raiders. The Italians were able to harvest their crops and live in peace. For the first time in many years, they had security and unity. Besides, the Lombards did not interfere with Italian laws or try to make them give up their Catholic Christianity.

For many years, the Lombards kept to themselves. As a warrior people, they did not try to meet and be friendly with the people

they had conquered. But this slowly changed.

To help understand how the Lombards and the Italians mingled and became one, and the part religion played in this, we will follow the story of an imaginary Lombard warrior, Aldo, and an imaginary Italian woman, Licia.

At the beginning of our story, the Lombards just fought off a raid by the Franks, thus earning again the gratitude of the Italians in their duchy. The Lombards planned a victory celebration, and they invited the Italians living nearby.

Joining in a celebration with the Lombards was quite a change for the Italians. But many of them decided to forget their distrust and to meet peacefully with the Lombards.

Licia and her father, a farmer, came to the feast. She carried a jar of wine, her father's gift. Licia's father was a fervent Christian and had brought up all of his children to be strong in the Christian faith.

Aldo, a Lombard warrior, saw Licia at the feast, and he could not help staring at her. He wanted to forget that he was a Lombard and go over to the Italians to talk with Licia's father so that he could be closer to the young woman. Licia saw that Aldo was staring at her. She was surprised and wondered what to do, but she said nothing. Aldo also said nothing, but he decided to visit her family.

4. Some of the Lombards were Arian Christians, and some were pagans. They learned more about Catholic Christianity, but their rulers forbade them to become Catholics.

Now we continue our imaginary story about Aldo and Licia. Aldo visited Licia's family and spent time talking with her father. He was interested in the stories that her father told about the history of the Roman people, who had settled this area hundreds of years ago.

Aldo saw, too, how much this Christian family believed in someone they called Jesus Christ, the Son of God. He saw that they felt united with Jesus and with each other. When he ate a meal with them, he sat in silence, wondering, as they prayed together before they ate.

Aldo was a pagan, but many other Lombards were Arian Christians. As Arians, they did not believe that Jesus Christ was truly God. They believed that Jesus did not have a divine nature, but that he was a created being whom God adopted as his Son by a special act of grace. But all this meant little to Aldo because he was a pagan. He really knew nothing about Christian beliefs.

Aldo spent more and more time with

Licia's family. One day, he and some of his Lombard friends asked Licia's older brother to take them fishing. Usually, Lombards did not mingle with the Italians, but they were beginning to find out that the Italians could show them many new and good things.

Licia's brother took the Lombards to freshwater streams and showed them where to find hardshelled creatures, called crustaceans, that lived in the water. The Lombards enjoyed the trip, and later, Licia cooked the crustaceans in a way that was new to the Lombards. It was a happy party.

Afterward, Aldo told Licia that he loved her and that he planned to ask her father to let her marry him. Some other Italian women had married Lombards, and Aldo thought that there would be no problem. But Licia told him that her father would never let her marry him. And she would not ask her father to let her marry Aldo because she was a Catholic Christian and he was a pagan.

Aldo was surprised. Lombard law forbade Lombards from becoming Catholic Christians or letting their children be baptized as Catholics. If they disobeyed, they would lose their rights as Lombards. So when a Lombard man married an Italian woman, the woman had to become an Arian Christian or a pagan, like her husband. Aldo had thought that Licia would become a pagan. But Licia said she would never give up her Christian faith.

What could Aldo do? If he became a Catholic Christian, Licia would marry him, but he could no longer be a Lombard! It was a terrible problem, and he had to think seriously about it.

5. The Lombard queen, a friend of Pope Gregory I, became a Catholic Christian, and other Lombard rulers were converted. Soon a new law was made: Lombards could become Catholics.

The law that forbade Lombards to become Catholic Christians had been made by King Authari. He died in 590, and his widow, Queen Theodolinda, married Duke Agilulf of Turin, who became king of the Lombards.

Queen Theodolinda was friendly with Pope Gregory I, and she became more and more interested in the Catholic faith. She and her husband came to believe that Jesus Christ was truly God, and that Catholic Christianity was the true faith.

Some of the Lombard dukes followed the example of the king and queen and became Catholic Christians. Licia and Aldo, in our

imaginary story, lived in a duchy ruled by a duke who converted to Catholic Christianity.

One day, this duke sent a message to his people about a new law: Lombards could become Catholic Christians.

Aldo could hardly believe it. Now he could become a Catholic and marry Licia; and he could still keep all his rights as a Lombard. He hurried to tell Licia the good news. He thought that all he had to do was be baptized, and then her father would let them get married.

But Licia told him that she did not want him to become a Catholic Christian unless he really believed that Jesus was the Son of God. She wanted him to learn about Christianity, and to believe with all his heart. Aldo was ready to give up. He thought that he might just forget all about marrying Licia. He was a warrior. He didn't have time to learn about the Christian religion.

Licia and her family did not give up. They asked him to give Christianity a chance, to talk to someone who could explain it to him. And so Aldo talked to Arnulf, a Lombard who had become a Christian and was now a deacon of the Church. Arnulf began to explain Christianity to Aldo.

6. Lombards began to give up their old religions. As the years passed, they became part of the Italian people, bringing Italy new strength. Today Lombardy, a part of Italy, is named after them.

Aldo, the Lombard in our imaginary story, was instructed in the Christian religion by Arnulf, a Lombard who had become a deacon in the Catholic Church. Arnulf explained to Aldo that the Church is a community or family of Christians, and that Christ is always present in that community, even if he cannot be seen with human eyes.

Aldo could understand this a little because he felt the unity and love in Licia's family. He knew that somehow Christ was with them. Gradually Aldo came to believe that the man called Jesus Christ was the Son of God—that he was crucified, was raised from the dead, and was now present in the Christian community.

Licia and her father saw that Aldo now wanted to be baptized because he truly wanted to become a Christian. And so, one happy day, Aldo and a small group of other Lombards were baptized in a small stream.

Aldo, Licia, and her family are imaginary, but the events that happened are really true. Around the year 590, many Lombard dukes gave their people permission to become Catholics, and many of these people were baptized.

And it is true that as the years went on, the ties between the Italians and Lombards became closer. Lombard law became based on older Roman law. The Lombard kings and dukes helped the Church. They built monasteries and encouraged development of art. Bishops were given more power, and they became local rulers as well as spiritual leaders.

There is something magnificent about the story of the Lombards. They came as a warrior people to a land that suffered from constant wars and invasions. Though they themselves were invaders, they stayed to become part of the country, and to learn to accept its culture and religion. By becoming part of Italy, they made Italy partly Lombard for all time to come. Today, a region of Italy—Lombardy—is named after them.

7. Gregory, a young man from a noble family, held a high office in Rome in 573. Suddenly he gave up his job and became a monk. He turned his fine home into a monastery.

By the middle of the sixth century, it probably was difficult to find many true natives of Rome in that city. People had come from many parts of the world and settled in Rome. Meanwhile, many wealthy Romans preferred to live in their country homes, far away from the confusion and decay of the once great city. But some native Romans were still willing to remain in Rome and to take on the task of rebuilding and governing it.

One such person was a man named Gregory. He had been born around 540 into the Anici family, one of the noble families of Rome. His father was a senator of the city and a Christian. He admired the ancient greatness of Rome and wanted to restore Rome's place in the world. Gregory followed in his father's footsteps. After finishing his studies, he took up a career in the civil service of Rome. Perhaps he hoped to restore greatness to Rome by using Christian principles. If Rome had been a great city when its people followed pagan principles, why could it not be great when its people had faith in Jesus Christ?

Gregory devoted himself seriously to his work. By 573 he had been elected prefect of the city of Rome. This was the most important city office. People sought it eagerly because the prefect had charge of the city's funds and could easily make himself rich. But Gregory had other ideas. He spent public money to benefit the people who lived in the city. And he showed special concern for the needs of the many poor people in Rome. Soon the young prefect had won the respect and admiration of many Romans.

Yet Gregory was still not content with his way of life. He often thought about his mother, who spent her days in silence and prayer. Perhaps he wanted to imitate such a life of prayer. Around the year 574, Gregory stopped wearing the red toga of a Roman city official, gave up his office, and put on the lowly clothing of a monk. Many people were surprised and saddened. They begged Gregory to return to his job as prefect, but he would not change his mind. He had given up his office and his social position to live the poor and simple life of a monk.

Gregory had a home on one of the seven hills of Rome. There he settled down, welcoming other people who wanted to share the life of a monk with him. In a short time his home had become a real monastery. There people lived and prayed according to the example and rules of St. Benedict, whom Gregory greatly admired.

8. The pope called Gregory to leave the monastery and help him in the work of the Church. When the pope died, Gregory was chosen to replace him. He became a great pope, giving special thought and care to the poor and suffering.

Not many years after Gregory began to live the life of a monk, the pope sent for him. Rome was divided into seven districts or parishes, each one under the care of a deacon. Pope Pelagius II wanted Gregory to take charge of one of these parishes. Gregory did not want to leave his peaceful life as a monk, but he obeyed the pope's request. He once again became active in the problems of Rome, doing what he could to help the poorest people in the city.

Soon Pope Pelagius II called Gregory to work by his side as his personal adviser and assistant. Around 578, the pope sent Gregory to Constantinople as his ambassador. One of the purposes of Gregory's mission was to get the aid of the emperor and the Byzantines against the Lombards. Gregory remained in Constantinople for seven years. He was not successful in getting help from the emperor for the pope. Misunderstandings and disputes between Rome and Constantinople made Gregory's job even harder. Gregory may have begun to feel that the Roman Church would have to find its own way to solve its problems—that it could not count on help from the emperor.

When Gregory returned to Rome in 586, he was able to enjoy the peaceful, quiet life of his monastery for a short time. Then, in 590, Pope Pelagius II died. The people of Rome insisted that Gregory become pope. He did all he could to avoid accepting this difficult of-

fice, but he finally recognized that the pleas of the people were the will of God. On September 3, 590, he was crowned as pope.

During this period, the pope did not have only religious duties. He also had to concern himself with the problems of the city of Rome, which were many and serious. More than once in the past, barbarian peoples had invaded Italy and looted Rome. Right now

the Lombards threatened to capture and destroy the city. Natural disasters had also brought much death and destruction. In 589 the Tiber River had overflowed and flooded the city, killing many people, destroying houses and monuments, and washing away food supplies. Famine and plague followed.

In the face of these disasters, Gregory did a huge amount of work. He worked to make peace with the Lombards. He ordered that there be prayers and processions throughout the city to ask for God's help. He placed the goods of the Church at the disposal of the poor. Gregory himself took great personal interest in the poor, whom he often invited to meals in his own home. He really considered himself to be "the servant of the servants of God," which is how he signed his letters.

9. Pope Gregory I wanted to spread the Christian message to people in the western part of what had once been the Roman empire. He sent out missionaries. One of the most famous was Augustine, who went to England in 596.

When he became pope, Gregory did not forget that he had lived the life of a monk. He admired St. Benedict and had modeled his monastery after that of this saint. Gregory wrote a life of St. Benedict, which we can read today. He also wrote sermons and books about the duty of pastors. These writings were read for many centuries. Gregory is looked upon as the fourth great teacher of the western Church. The other three are St. Ambrose, St. Jerome, and St. Augustine.

Gregory kept careful track of the Church lands in Italy. And he was concerned about the future of the western Church in a very changed world. Closer ties would have to be formed with the various Germanic peoples who now controlled parts of the old Roman empire in the West. The pope would also have to gain better control over local bishops and churches in order to maintain unity and to bring the Gospel message to life among them. Christianity could help to civilize people in the West, and Gregory felt that the papacy—that is, the government of the pope—should take charge of that task. For his many efforts, Gregory is regarded as one of the first great popes of the Middle Ages. He is known to us as Gregory the Great, who began the work of making the papacy a real center of

power and influence in Europe. Much that happened in western Europe during the next few centuries can be traced back to the efforts of Gregory.

One of Pope Gregory's famous projects was the mission he sent to England to convert the Anglo-Saxons. In 596, forty monks, led by Gregory's friend Augustine, left his monastery and boarded ship at Ostia. Their goal was England, and in those days the journey was long and difficult.

In the spring of 597 the monks landed in England. The country was divided into many small states, each ruling itself. Augustine decided to approach the king of Kent—Aethelbert—who was supposed to be friendly toward Christianity. He went to Canterbury, where the king lived, and he was quite successful. In 601, Aethelbert became a Christian, and many of his subjects followed his example. Pope Gregory appointed Augustine as the bishop of Canterbury, and Canterbury has remained the first and most important episcopal see, or cathedral city, in England. From there Augustine and his monks carried on successful missionary activity in other parts of England. The dreams of Gregory were beginning to turn into reality.

10. At this time, Spain was ruled by the Visigoths. A struggle took place between Catholic Christians and Arian Christians. The fight ended in 587, when the Visigothic king became a Catholic.

The Visigoths had invaded Spain, and by the sixth century, they controlled most of it. They were Arian Christians, but many of the natives of Spain were Catholic Christians. At first this difference in religious belief had not caused great difficulty, because the Visigoths lived apart from the native population. The people were allowed to follow their religion in peace.

As time went on, however, Visigoths became interested in the local culture, and

many of them became Catholic Christians. The Visigothic kings and nobles began to fear that their rule would be weakened if their people gave up the Arian religion. When King Leovigild came to the throne, he wanted to insure the unity of his kingdom. He decided to solve the religious problem once and for all.

At a council held in Toledo in 580, he tried to get rid of some of the most disputed beliefs of Arianism. Then he tried to make Arian Christianity the only religion of his land. He attempted this by forbidding Arians to become Catholic Christians and by promising a better life to Catholics who became Arians.

People reacted strongly against Leovigild's decree. One of the king's own sons, who was a Catholic Christian, led a revolt against the king. Leovigild defeated his son's revolt and had him executed, but his victory did not last long. When Leovigild died, his son Recared became king. In 587, Recared was converted to Catholic Christianity, and many of his subjects followed his example. Some Visigothic nobles who clung to Arianism revolted, but Recared won out. Close ties developed with the Roman Church and its clergy, and Visigothic Spain enjoyed a brief time of peace and glory before the invasion of the Muslims.

11. Spain now had a time
of religious peace.
The Church grew stronger.
Learning and education
became more important.
Isidore of Seville wrote
an encyclopedia
of knowledge that was
studied for many years.

Once peace and religious unity had been restored to some extent in Spain, the Visigothic kingdom entered a brief period of revival. Native Spanish Christians and Christian Visigoths benefited from the new, stronger role of the Church in Spain. But serious problems of leadership, particularly by the Visigothic kings, remained. Spain would fall quickly to the Muslims in the early years of the eighth century.

In the seventh century, however, there was a revival of learning to some extent. In Spain, some people tried to combine knowledge from the Greek and Roman past with Christian teaching. And they tried to connect all this to the traditions of the native population and their Visigothic rulers.

One of the most active and learned men of this time was Isidore, who was born in Spain

into a Spanish-Roman family in the second half of the sixth century. An eager student, he felt that it was possible to preserve learning for the people of his land. When he became bishop of Seville in 600, he started the huge task of collecting knowledge and writing it down in books for students and others. Isidore wrote on many subjects, dictating to many secretaries what he had learned.

His most famous work is the *Etymologies*, which can be regarded as the first Christian encyclopedia. In it, Isidore wrote down everything he had learned from reading earlier authors: ancient learning, Christian teaching, grammar, arithmetic, geography, history, and so on. His work was greatly admired by the people of his day, and it was carefully studied for many centuries.

Isidore lived and wrote during a time when many people had no chance to get an education. He struggled to help people overcome ignorance, and today we admire his educational work. Yet we must realize that his encyclopedia was full of mistakes because general knowledge in Isidore's time was very limited.

One of Isidore's works that is still important and helpful today is his history of the Goths. Also, he finished a missal—the book of Bible readings used at Mass—and a breviary, or prayerbook, for priests. Both of these had been left unfinished by another author. Because of his zeal for spreading knowledge, Isidore is now called a Doctor of the Church.

12. Irish monks spread the faith in Ireland, and their monasteries became centers of learning. St. Columbanus, a famous Irish monk, left Ireland in 596 to build a monastery in Luxeuil, in the land we now call France.

Christianity had been introduced into Ireland around 430 by St. Patrick, a bishop. Irish monks preserved the faith there, spreading it and studying it more deeply. Large monasteries often led to the development of villages and towns nearby because peasants, colonists, and whole families would settle in the neighborhood.

The monasteries had schools where the Christian faith and the learning of the day were taught to children and young people, who often lived in the monasteries. Thus the monks were in touch with their people and sought to better their people's lives. And the Irish monks of this period were noted for their learning, which surpassed that of most Europeans on the continent.

One particular achievement of the Irish monks was the introduction of individual, private Confession. Up until then, Confession had been a public, group matter. The Irish monks thought that a private, personal talk between priest and penitent could be more beneficial. The Irish monks also encouraged pilgrimages and took such trips themselves to venerate the relics of martyrs and other saints.

Columbanus, perhaps the most famous Irish monk, left Ireland in 590 with twelve companions to make a pilgrimage on the continent of Europe. In the land of the Franks, however, he found a sad situation. The Christians there were very ignorant. Local priests and other clerics could not improve the situation. Columbanus decided to settle there and help his fellow Christians. With the help of the ruler and the religious authorities, he built a great monastery in Luxeuil. Besides quarters for the monks, it had large guest quarters for people who wanted to share the life of the monks for a while or to study there. Another large room was the refectory—the dining room, where monks and guests ate their meals together. The monastery also had a school where the more learned monks taught. Thus began a flourishing center of religious life and learning in Luxeuil, providing civil and cultural improvement of the people in what we know today as France.

13. The monastery founded by Columbanus in Luxeuil became a great center of religion, study, and teaching. People came to Luxeuil for both spiritual and material help, and to go to Confession.

After the monastery of Luxeuil was built, Columbanus wanted to make sure that it would display the same spirit of seriousness and hard work that could be found in Irish monasteries. He made great demands on his monks. Instead of frightening people away, however, his demands attracted many sincere and generous Christians into the monastic way of life. Luxeuil soon became a large community with many monks, and other monasteries had to be built.

Sound organization was one of the things that impressed people about Luxeuil. In the monastery school, Columbanus and other learned monks taught future monks and lay people. Their teaching was excellent, and soon Frankish noblemen were eager to send

their sons to school at Luxeuil. The noblemen also gave land and other gifts to the monastery. The fields were farmed by monks and peasants. One monk was in charge of all this work, and he had to make sure that there was food for the monks, the students, the peasants, and the many poor people who might come for help. Almost everything needed by the monks was prepared in the monastery, which had its own cooks, bakers, tailors, and other skilled workers and craftsmen.

Some of the monks took care of the needs of the faithful. Many lay people came to the monastery to get advice or to go to Confession. And the monks often went into the nearby villages to preach to the people and teach them. The people were often poor and very uneducated, and they had great affection for the holy, energetic monks.

As time went on, some members of the nobility, both lay people and church officials, began to envy the monks. They were afraid that the good example of the monks would lead to a loss of their own prestige and privileges. When it was necessary, the monks criticized the unchristian behavior of certain lords and even bishops. Indeed, an argument with a bishop forced Columbanus himself to leave Luxeuil. But his work was carried on, and so Christian life in the kingdom of the Franks was permanently improved by Irish monks.

14. Other monks heard of Columbanus's work and followed his example. Amandus, from Aquitaine, was inspired to preach the Gospel of Christ to the Flemish people. He is now known as the Apostle of Flanders.

The example of Columbanus and the Irish monks soon became known throughout the Christian areas of Europe. Many Christians tried to imitate Columbanus. One of his most famous followers was Amandus, a devout Christian from the French region of Aquitaine.

Amandus had been living the life of a hermit near the city of Bourges. In 640 he set out on a pilgrimage to the tomb of the apostles Peter and Paul in Rome. While Amandus was praying in the Church of St. Peter, we are told that he had a vision. The apostle Peter appeared to him and told him to preach the Gospel message in the Belgian region of Flanders, where there were still many pa-

gans. Amandus set out at once for Flanders and stopped in the town of Maastricht, which today is in the country of Holland, near the Belgian border. Amandus preached the Gospel so lovingly and devoutly in Maastricht that he was soon acclaimed bishop by the faithful.

Amandus, however, had not planned to settle down forever in one city. After a few years, he left Maastricht to proclaim Jesus and his message to other Flemish towns and villages in what is now Belgium. Those living in this area were plain and simple people who lived by fishing. Many of them had never even heard of Jesus Christ. Amandus went into their fishing villages and proclaimed the Gospel, often at the risk of being killed by ruthless, excited pagans. He would leave one of his followers in charge of the Christian community in the village when he moved on. In this way he built up a series of mission stations stretching from Maastricht and Ghent to Antwerp. He often visited the towns and villages, urging Christians to live their faith properly and inspiring them by his own example.

Amandus received many gifts from well-to-do families. He used these gifts to ransom slaves, offering them freedom and faith in Jesus Christ. When Amandus died in 676, the conversion of Belgium was ensured. And so he has been called the Apostle of Flanders.

15. In the seventh century, the Byzantine empire was faced with many problems. It was under attack by Persians and Arabs. Also, Christians disputed the true nature of Jesus Christ. A great monk, Maximus the Confessor, spoke out for the truth.

While monks and others were beginning to spread faith and culture to the peoples in western Europe, the Byzantine empire in the East was going through a period of crises. It was threatened from the outside by Persians and Arabs, who were invading its territory. It was threatened from the inside by arguments and divisions between Christians themselves. Many of these arguments were about the nature of Jesus Christ. These disagreements went back to the time of earlier church councils, which had decided that Jesus was both God and a human being and that he had both a divine nature and a human nature.

This view was challenged by some groups of Christians who held that Jesus was only divine and not human. These two opposing views caused continuing division between Christians in the Byzantine empire. And the unity of the empire was threatened even more when the Muslims began to capture provinces that had once belonged to the Byzantine empire.

The emperor, Constantius II, wanted to stop the religious disagreements and unify his country. He decreed that Jesus had only one will, and then he forbade all discussion about the matter. He thought people would accept this compromise, but many Christians felt that the truths of their faith were so very important that they had to speak out against the emperor's law.

One of the great defenders of the truth was a learned monk named Maximus, who would later be called the Confessor. Maximus had held an important office in the emperor's service but had given it up to become a monk. Now he became the leader of those Christians who believed that Jesus Christ was both God and man. Maximus asked Pope Martin I for help. At a meeting of the leaders of the Church held in Rome in 649, Maximus's views were upheld.

The emperor had threatened to punish people who challenged his order. He kept his word. Pope Martin I was taken prisoner and dragged off to Constantinople. There he was tried for treason, badly mistreated, and banished to the Crimea. A year or two later (655 or 656) Pope Martin died in the Crimea. Maximus had fled to Africa, but he was captured and brought to Constantinople.

16. Maximus was imprisoned for his beliefs, but he continued to defend the truth taught by the Church. The emperor had Maximus tortured, trying to make him give up his beliefs. This holy monk died in prison.

After being taken to Constantinople, Maximus was tried by men who agreed with the emperor. They ordered him to accept the emperor's decree and to give up his own beliefs. But Maximus was sure that the emperor was wrong. The council of Chalcedon, he said, had declared that Jesus had two natures: a divine nature and a human nature. How could Jesus have saved us if he were not both God and man? If Jesus were only God, he could not have taken our sins upon himself and died for us on the cross. If Jesus were only a human being, he could not have made up for our sins.

Since Jesus had two natures, said Maximus, he must also have had two wills: a divine will and a human will. If Jesus had only a divine will, then he would not have been a complete and perfect human being. Yet Christians believed that he was indeed a complete and perfect human being. Maximus went on to point out that Jesus' human will was perfectly obedient to the will of God. Maximus loved to cite the story of Jesus' agony in the garden of Gethsemane. There Jesus had asked his heavenly Father to spare him from suffering. But then he had added: "Not my will but thine be done."

The judges ruled that Maximus had to obey the emperor. They also accused Maximus of being friendly with a man named Gregory, who had set himself up as emperor in opposition to the emperor in Constantinople.

Constantius II, the real emperor, was an able and good ruler in many respects. He tried hard to stop the advance of the Muslim Arabs and to restore strength to the Byzantine empire. But he made a serious mistake in this debate over Christian truth, and he badly mistreated Maximus. The emperor had Maximus tortured and then condemned to exile. But Maximus refused to keep silent, and he was arrested and brought to Constantinople a second time. There he died in 662 from the wounds and tortures inflicted on him.

In death, however, Maximus proved to be the victor. His teaching about the two natures of Christ won fairly rapid acceptance, and today it is held by the Roman Catholic Church. Maximus himself was declared a saint and a confessor because he had not been afraid to bear witness to Christian truth with his own life.

17. A serious religious dispute
arose in the early part
of the eighth century.
Many Christians venerated
images of Jesus, Mary,
and the saints. But now
some wanted to destroy
all religious images
because they feared that
Christians might begin
to worship images instead
of worshiping God.
In 726, Emperor Leo III
decided to do away
with religious images.

The very first Christians rarely made religious pictures or statues. Influenced by the Jewish background of Christianity, they thought one could not show the invisible God in an image. In those days, statues of pagan gods were still in buildings and on monuments. Christians feared that making religious images might lead Christians into idolatry—the worship of statues as gods. But as time went on, it became common for Christians to make images of Jesus, Mary, and the saints, particularly after Christianity became the official religion of the Roman empire. There no longer seemed to be any danger of confusing Christian images with those of pagan gods.

By the seventh century, the use of religious images—called icons by Greek-speaking Christians—was widespread. Monks, in particular, supported and encouraged people when they used such images to help them with their prayers. But some Christians were worried about the ever growing use of such religious images. They may have felt that such use might lead to idolatry. They may have been influenced by the rise and spread of Islam, which forbade images.

The people who opposed the use of images or icons were called iconoclasts, which meant image breakers. Those who favored their use for prayer were called iconodules. When Leo III became the Byzantine emperor in 717, the position of the iconoclasts was greatly strengthened. A smart and energetic ruler, he successfully defended Constantinople against the Arabs (717-718) and reigned until 741. Around 726, Leo began to do away with the use of images. In fact, he set an example by removing a famous image of Christ from his palace.

Reaction to his attack on images was strong and widespread. People revolted in several places. Byzantine rule began to fall apart in the regions of Italy still held by the emperor. The patriarch of Constantinople spoke in favor of images, and so did the pope in Rome.

Leo III, however, was not going to give in. He put down the revolts and issued a law forbidding the use of images throughout his empire. It seemed that the iconoclasts were going to win out. But in the years ahead, the faith of the common people would prevail.

18. John of Damascus offered a clear view about the proper use of religious images and helped settle the dispute. John had been the Christian representative to the Muslims, but he gave this up in 726 to become a monk. He spent the rest of his life in prayer and study. John was greatly admired as a writer and thinker.

John of Damascus, also known as John Damascene, was born around 675 in the city of Damascus, Syria. At that time, the city was the home of the caliph—the ruler of the Muslim peoples. Christians were encouraged to become Muslims, but the rulers treated Christians fairly well. Indeed, Christians had their own representative in the court of the caliph. This representative was a civil official who presented the views of the Christian community to the caliph and who reported Arab demands and laws to his fellow Christians. John's father held this office, and John himself took it over when his father died.

In 726, however, John resigned his office to enter a monastery in Palestine, near Jerusalem. He became a monk and dedicated himself to prayer and study. John wrote in a beautiful Greek style, and several of his works were admired as masterpieces. One such work was entitled *On the Orthodox Faith*, and it was much used in the Middle Ages. Even today it is a valuable source for the opinions of many earlier Church Fathers who lived in the East. John also helped to encourage painting, liturgy, and hymns in the Byzantine Church.

In the quiet of his monastery, John heard about the debate over the use of images. He had great devotion for an icon of Mary that was venerated in his monastery, and he could not understand why some Christians wanted to destroy all such images. But he examined all the arguments against images and prayed for guidance on the issue.

Around 740, John began to publish writings about religious images. When Christians venerate images, he said, they are not venerating the wood or the other material of which the images are made. They are paying respect to the persons or events represented by the images. So the images help people to recall the virtuous life of Jesus, Mary, and the saints; and the images also inspire people to imitate these holy figures.

These simple, straightforward ideas, presented in the fine style that was typical of John, made a deep impression on people. When he died in 749, he was admired as the greatest defender of icons. By the middle of the next century, the controversy over icons was finished, and John's view had won out.

19. Within one hundred years of Mohammed's death in 632, the followers of Islam had conquered lands all the way from the Atlantic Ocean to the Indian Ocean. They controlled the waterways and land routes in this whole area.

Within a hundred years of the death of Mohammed, the Muslims had created a vast empire. The ruler of the Muslim world, the caliph of Damascus, controlled territories extending from Spain and North Africa on the Atlantic Ocean to northern India. The great centers of Christianity on the eastern and southern shores of the Mediterranean Sea were under Muslim rule, except for Constantinople and its greatly reduced empire. The Muslims controlled the Mediterranean, the Red Sea, and the approaches to the Indian Ocean. The great waterways and highways of commerce in that whole area were in their hands. This geographical position would lead to the flowering of a great civilization during the next few centuries.

20. The civilization of the people of Islam, or Muslims, grew and developed greatly. They built beautiful cities, which became centers of education, trade, and Muslim spiritual life.

By the middle of the eighth century, Damascus was no longer the capital of the Islamic world. Muslim rule was now divided. Muslims remained united in their religion and their civilization, but they no longer had one sole supreme ruler. While most Muslims still respected the caliph in Damascus as the symbol of Muslim unity, they did not look to him as their political ruler.

The Muslims built a great new city, Baghdad, on the banks of the Tigris River in the Middle East. The region of the Tigris and Euphrates Rivers was a meeting place for the traffic and commerce of the whole world: from Europe and the Mediterranean Sea to the Indian Ocean, India, and China; and from the coast of Africa to the heartland of Asia. Muslim commerce grew greatly. Muslim ships traveled the Indian Ocean, establishing trading posts as far away as Korea and China. The trade of the Mediterranean Sea was almost entirely in Muslim hands, though it should be remembered that the traders and sailors might be Greeks, Jews, Syrians, Africans, or some other race or nationality living under Muslim rule.

The Islamic faith was studied more deeply and developed. Its orthodox or established version was the Sunni version. This was based on the Koran, the traditions or doctrinal pronouncements attributed to Mohammed, and later religious, moral, and social laws. The caliph was supposed to be the defender of the orthodox religion, but in fact this task was soon taken over by a group of religious teachers in each local region. These teachers were known as *ulema*, and they played a role similar to that of the rabbis in Judaism. There were also other versions of Islam, the most well known being the Shiite version. At that time, the main difference between the Sunni and the Shiite Muslims was their belief about their ruler or caliph. The Sunni believed that the caliph could be elected, and the Shiite believed that he must be descended from the one appointed by Mohammed.

Numerous cities were built or rebuilt under the Muslim rule. These cities served as centers of administration and learning. They promoted religious education, commerce, and devotion to Islam—which means submission to Allah. Every big city had at least one mosque—the Muslim house of prayer—which also served as a center of social life in the Muslim community. The vitality of Islam could be seen in the beautiful buildings and flourishing activity of these cities. There were Baghdad and Samarra on the Tigris River, Córdoba and Almería in Spain, Fez in Morocco, and, somewhat later, Palermo in Sicily.

21. Islamic civilization was strong in its cities. There people from many nations shared knowledge and writings. From this study and sharing came an original Islamic culture. Schools, libraries, and centers for research were built. Important advances were made in science, mathematics, and medicine.

Besides being centers of government and commerce, Islamic cities were places where people from many lands and cultures met and mingled. They exchanged goods, ideas, and cultural knowledge. The geographical position of the Islamic world enabled it to be a meeting point for many different cultures. During this period Islamic rulers and their courts tended to favor such interchanges.

In Baghdad, for example, the ideas and discoveries of many cultures came together. India offered its mathematics, and in particular, the use of the zero for mathematical operations. Persia offered its royal and governmental practices; it had once been one of the first truly cosmopolitan kingdoms. Greece and the later Hellenistic-Oriental world around the time of Christ provided its

philosophy. And all of these cultures contributed knowledge that had been gathered about medicine, astronomy, and geography.

The vast effort of translating foreign works into Arabic made this knowledge available to Islamic students and scholars. The Muslims built schools, libraries, and centers for research. They wrote the first treatments of what we know as mathematics, and they gave algebra the name it still has today. They developed the study of plants, crop planting, and irrigation. Much attention was given to medicine. Al-Razi (865-925), director of the state hospital in Baghdad, was involved in many practical medical projects, wrote many books, and devised the first scientific treatment of smallpox. Many other Islamic scholars made great contributions to general learning. Islamic theology was also developed.

During this period, then, the Islamic world was anxious to learn new things and to meet the world around it. Some Muslims were afraid that this tendency would lead to a loss of the original faith of Islam. Other Muslims thought that they should keep opening up to new ideas and influences from the outside. But all agreed that people had to be educated. Many scholars came from all over the Muslim world to study at the main centers of learning. If it had not been for their work, much of the science and learning that Europeans studied in the later Middle Ages might not have been available at all.

22. Throughout Europe,
barbarian tribes had
established their cities
and kingdoms.
Germanic tribes
had spread through
western Europe, and
Slavic peoples populated
eastern Europe.

Throughout Europe—except where the Byzantine emperor still had some small control—barbarian tribes had taken control of the land. Germanic tribes ruled most regions of western Europe, and Slavic tribes occupied eastern Europe. A brief look at Germanic tribal life will give us some idea of European society during the period between the Baptism of Clovis (496) and the rise of the Carolingian Franks in the eighth century.

The tribes owned the land and resources of the areas they occupied. Property was distributed to, or shared in some way by, all the free men who had been born or adopted into the tribe. Earlier inhabitants of a conquered area became the subjects of the conquerors. They had to work the land, share their harvest with the new rulers, and obey the laws of these rulers.

The ruler of a tribal region, who might today be called king, earned his high position

by his strong military leadership. The tribal king had to be able to win the respect and loyalty of other warriors. He was often elected by the assembly of free men in the tribe, who picked the man they felt to be most worthy. By this time, there was a tendency to choose a worthy man from within the family of the previous ruler. But as yet, the oldest son of a king did not automatically become king at his father's death. Germanic custom had established the idea that a man had to be worthy to rule, and that the tribal assembly of free men should choose this ruler.

Other military leaders, now often called dukes, shared the king's power. They were the king's captains in warfare, and often they ruled and managed part of the tribe's land.

The law in force was that of the tribe or clan, together with some customs of the region and some elements of Roman law. Most of the Roman laws were now replaced by Germanic laws of a rather crude type. To enforce local law and administer districts, counts were appointed by the ruler. In some places, the Germanic custom of trial by physical ordeal—by fire or water or fighting—became a common way to decide if a person was guilty or innocent.

Social life was based to a large extent on personal ties—ties to the king, to a local count or duke, to the owner of one's land, and to one's relatives. Commerce and outside trade were relatively unimportant. Salt was one of the few basic necessities acquired by trade. Agriculture was the main local occupation of most people. As time passed, even the free Germanic men, who saw themselves primarily as warriors, began to sink to the same social class as the local non-Germans—that is, to become peasants. Power and wealth were enjoyed by fewer and fewer people.

23. In the seventh century, the power of the ruling Merovingian Franks was challenged by Pepin of Landen, who began to gain control of Merovingian lands. This control was strengthened by his descendants, and the Merovingian king became almost powerless. This was the beginning of a new era in western Europe.

When Clovis, a Merovingian Frank, was baptized in 496, strong ties seemed to be assured between the Church of Rome and at least one powerful Germanic people. But rivalries between the Franks and weakening power of the ruling family, the Merovingians, prevented any strong alliance.

This situation began to change in the early part of the seventh century. A powerful landlord in the eastern part of the Merovingian kingdom, known as Austrasia, gained control of the king's finances. This landlord, Pepin of Landen, became the main official of the king's government, or Mayor of the Palace. He was also the head of the king's army. Pepin gradually established ties with, and lordship over, other Franks. (Pepin's family later became the ruling family among the Franks and was known as the Carolingians.)

In 687, Pepin's grandson, Pepin of Herstal, gained control of the entire kingdom that used to be ruled by the Merovingian kings. This control was made even stronger by Charles Martel, the son of Pepin of Herstal. Though there still was a Merovingian king, he really was almost powerless.

In Poitiers, in 732, Charles Martel defeated the army of Islamic Moors who were trying to move into Gaul from Spain. It was an important victory for him and the Christian West. Combined with the failure of the Muslims to capture Constantinople in the East and the internal troubles of the Muslim rule, or caliphate, in Damascus, this victory stopped the Muslims from advancing through Europe. It gave Christians in Europe some breathing space for their own development.

The popes were among the first to try to take advantage of this breathing space. At the time, the big debate over images was causing much ill will between Rome and the Byzantine emperor. Moreover, Lombard power was reaching its height in Italy under Liutprand, who was perhaps the greatest Lombard king. He united much of Italy under the Lombards and adopted measures for running the government that may have been borrowed by Charlemagne later. The popes, however, wanted support from orthodox Christian rulers, and the new Frankish leaders seemed perfectly suited for this.

Pope Gregory III (731-741) asked Charles Martel to come to his aid in Italy, but Charles refused. In 751, however, the son of Charles Martel was more open to papal pleas. That part of the Church's story and its outcome will be told later.

Bretons
Aachen
Paris
Poitiers
Kingdom
of the Franks
Bavarians
Saxons
Slavs
Lombards

24. In England, the Church grew strong during the seventh century. Monasteries and schools were built. Bede, a very learned monk, was the most important teacher and writer of this time. He wrote a history of the English people and told how they became Christian.

In the late sixth century, Italian monks were sent by Pope Gregory the Great to bring the Gospel message to England. The English Church grew steadily, as nobles and the people under their rule converted to Christianity. The Italian monks and the Irish monks both expanded their influence in England, but these two groups had different views about church organization and procedure, among other things. At an important synod—or church meeting—in 664 (the synod of Whitby), English churchmen decided to accept the rule of the Roman Church. This meant that Benedictine monasticism, which was so very strong in Rome, would prevail in England over the Irish form of monasticism.

One sign of growth in the English Church was a cultural revival. Bishop Benedict Biscop, a native Anglo-Saxon, founded the great monastery of Jarrow in Northumbria. He gave this monastery many books and art objects that he had brought from the European continent. Jarrow would become the

home of Bede, the monk who best symbolizes the revival of learning in England.

Bede was born in Northumbria in 673. His parents put him under the care of Bishop Biscop when he was seven. Bede went on to become a learned monk, and he was assigned to the monastery of Jarrow by the bishop. His life was not filled with exciting travels or heroic deeds. But his clear-minded teaching and his writings made an impression on people.

Bede's abbot asked him to write a history of the English people and their conversion to Christianity. That work, the *Ecclesiastical History of the English People*, proved to be an important, scholarly work, which still appeals to readers today. Bede carefully examined the library in his monastery and tried to be accurate in what he wrote. Beginning his story shortly before the birth of Jesus, he moved on to concentrate on the conversion of the English people and the important role that the Roman Church played in this.

In his history, Bede recounted a famous story about the conversion of the English. In 626 King Edwin assembled his advisers to help decide whether Northumbria should accept Christianity. One of his advisers had this to say: "O king, our life on earth seems to me like the flight of a bird. When you are sitting in the warmth of your home in the winter, a bird suddenly comes in one door and goes out the other. For the moment that the bird was indoors, the wind and cold could not touch it. But then it disappears in the dark night, and we don't know what happens to it. Well, we too feel secure during the brief space of our life; but then what? If this religion helps us to know what will happen after our life, we should accept it." After this little speech, the king's advisers took a vote and decided to become Christians.

Bede finished writing his history in 731 and died a few years later in Jarrow. For centuries he has been known as the Venerable Bede.

25. The Church in England
sent missionaries
to convert pagans living
on the continent
of Europe. A monk
named Willibrord was the
first of these missionaries.
Through such monks,
Pope Gregory the Great's
dream of a united, Christian
Europe was beginning
to come true!

Less than a century after Italian monks had brought the Gospel message to England, English monks were heading back to the continent to preach the Gospel to pagans in Europe. These missionaries were part of a well-organized and well-planned movement.

The first was a monk named Willibrord. Like Bede, he was a Northumbrian who entered a monastery at an early age. He also studied in Ireland but, unlike Bede, he did not feel called to a life of study and teaching. At the age of thirty, he was ordained a priest and

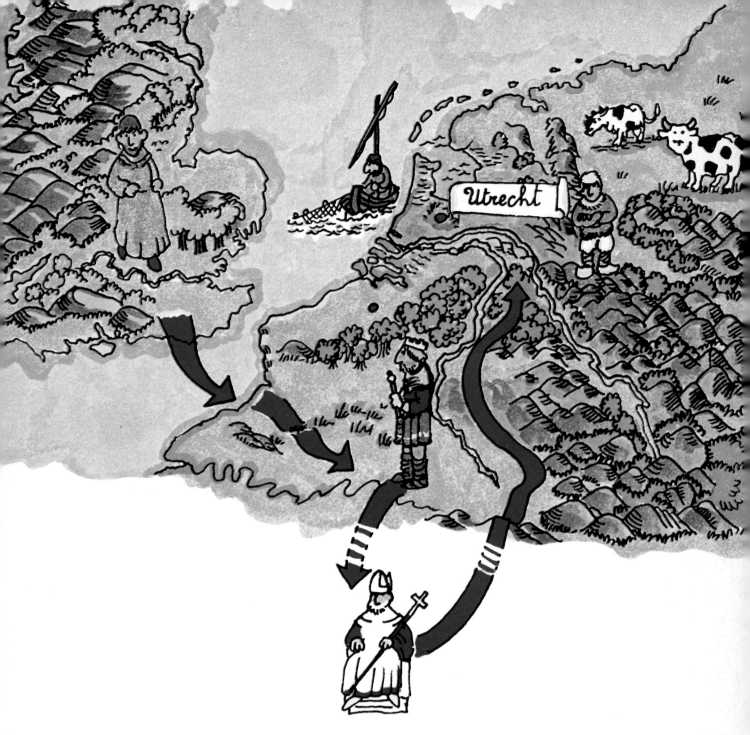

decided to become a missionary. Around 690 he and a few other monks were sent to Frisia, the area we know today as northern Holland, to proclaim the Gospel to the people there.

Willibrord was careful to plan his work. He made sure he got the support of Pepin of Herstal. Then, in 695, he went to Rome to get the backing of the pope. Pope Sergius consecrated him archbishop of the Frisians and gave him the name Clement.

After returning to Frisia, Willibrord continued to preach the Gospel there and in nearby lands. By the time he died in 739, Frisia had become a Christian land. In this way, the Christian history of Holland began.

In seeking the support of the pope and the Frankish leaders, Willibrord set an example that was later imitated by English missionaries with great success. The links of Christian community envisioned by Pope Gregory the Great a hundred years earlier were being forged into a strong chain. The work of Willibrord would be continued by his great successor, Winfrid.

26. Winfrid, another famous English monk, decided to become a missionary in 716. He wanted to preach the Gospel to the pagan Saxons, who lived in what is now Germany. Winfrid received the backing of the pope. And he took a new name—Boniface. After working with Willibrord for a time, Boniface left for Germany.

Though Willibrord began English missionary work on the continent of Europe, the outstanding missionary figure of this period was another English monk: Winfrid, who later became known as Boniface. Winfrid was born near the monastery of Exeter. At an early age he entered the monastery for studies. An admirer of Bede, Winfrid was a serious student. He became a priest and remained at the monastery as its director. He also taught, preached, and wrote books.

Winfrid felt a desire to bring the Gospel message to people who were ignorant of it. He had heard of the pagan Saxons—Germanic people who lived in what is now Germany—and he felt a strong desire to preach the Gospel to them. His attempt to reach the Saxons in 716 failed, but in 718 he tried again. This time he followed the sound example of Willibrord and went to Rome to see the pope before leaving on his mission. The pope received him favorably and gave him official permission to preach the Gospel. Winfrid had

his name changed to Boniface, an early Roman martyr. By taking this name, Winfrid showed his respect for the Church of Rome and his complete dedication to his mission.

Boniface then began his work of preaching the Gospel. He traveled far and wide in the regions of Germany known as Bavaria and Thuringia. He was preparing to move into the nearby regions when he learned that Willibrord needed his help in the north.

In Utrecht, King Radbod, an enemy of the Christians, had died. Willibrord felt that he could now preach the Gospel and convert people more easily, and that Boniface's help would speed up progress. The two missionaries were successful in a very short time. Boniface was such a great help that Willibrord wanted to make him his co-worker and successor. Gently but firmly, Boniface said no. His real aim was still the same: to bring the Gospel message to the Germanic Saxons living on the right bank of the Rhine River.

Frisia

Hesse

Thuringia

Bavaria

27. Boniface began his German mission in 721, in the region of Hesse. A year later, he was made a bishop and was given the task of organizing the Church throughout Germany. Boniface's work was supported by Charles Martel and by Martel's son, Carloman.

In 721 Boniface left Willibrord and the town of Utrecht to make another try at getting into Germanic territory. This time he was successful, and he managed to establish himself in the region of Hesse. There, with the help of local rulers, he was able to convert many pagans and to build a monastery.

The pope had asked to be kept informed of Boniface's progress, and so in 722, Boniface went to Rome, to report on his work. The pope consecrated Boniface a bishop, confirming his authority to preach to the Germanic pagans and to reorganize the churches existing in Germanic lands. This was an urgent task because many different churches had been established in Germanic lands east of the Rhine River. They had been founded at different times, had developed in isolation

Saxony

from one another, and had lost the authentic spirit of Christian living. Boniface took up the task willingly.

But it was no easy matter. Up to now he had preached mainly in pagan areas where no churches had been established. That did not bother too many Christians. But when he began to reorganize existing churches, to take away the special privileges of Christian bishops and noblemen, these people reacted sharply and angrily: "How dare this stranger jump in and decide what we should do! How dare he alter our practices and traditions! Why doesn't he go home where he belongs?"

Boniface did not allow himself to be discouraged by this unfavorable reaction. He established many monasteries and dioceses, and he held various councils to put through church reforms. He sought to establish contacts between churches, to restore good discipline, and to give a real Christian spirit to church officials and the faithful in Germanic regions.

Much of Boniface's work was carried on during the reign of Charles Martel, who supported his work. Boniface traveled throughout the Germanic regions, preaching the Gospel, establishing monasteries, and reforming local churches and dioceses. After Charles Martel died, one of his sons, Carloman, gave strong support to Boniface. Carloman had obviously been deeply influenced by his Christian upbringing, and in 747 he went to live in a monastery for the rest of his life.

28. After Charles Martel's death in 741, Boniface remained in the diocese of Mainz. His followers carried out his ideas and plans. Boniface continued to work for the Church. He had special concern for the English monks who had followed him to Europe. In 753 Boniface was killed by pagans while on a trip to Utrecht. He is known as the Apostle of Germany.

Boniface had met opposition from noblemen and even churchmen when he tried to reform the Church. That is probably one of the main reasons why he made sure that the monastery of Fulda, which he founded, was put directly under the control of the pope instead of under the local bishop.

Opposition to Boniface grew more bold after Charles Martel died in 741 and his son Carloman had withdrawn to a monastery. Charles's other son, Pepin, did not give Boniface the same wholehearted support. Boniface felt obliged to retire to his diocese of Mainz. But his ideas and plans remained alive, and they were carried out by his followers.

Boniface did not give way to discouragement. In Mainz he continued to work for his

flock. He showed special concern for the English monks who had joined him on the continent. Boniface often visited the monastery of Fulda, which he had founded in 744. He wanted it to become a great center of prayer, work, and learning like the monasteries in England or the great Benedictine monastery of Monte Cassino.

In 753 Boniface went to visit Utrecht. There the old missionary, now around eighty years old, was warmly welcomed by crowds of Christians. But some hostile pagans also decided to express their feelings about Boniface. They waylaid him as he and a band of Christians were on their way to give the sacrament of Confirmation to some new converts. Boniface was mortally wounded. As he was dying, he urged the Christians around him to remain faithful to the teaching of Jesus and to carry it out in their lives. Boniface's body was brought in triumph to Fulda. Ever since that time, he has been revered as the Apostle of Germany.

Boniface had made the Christian faith solid and strong in many parts of Germany. Now popes and Carolingian rulers together would form the first Christian empire in western Europe. The first steps would be taken by Charles Martel's son, Pepin. The important work of forming this empire would be carried through by Pepin's son, Charles, known to us as Charlemagne. His name in its Latin form—Carolus—plus the last part of the name Merovingian formed a new family name: Carolingian.

29. Closer ties were now formed between the Carolingian Franks and the papacy. Pepin III, the son of Charles Martel, was anointed as king of the Franks by Pope Stephen II. Pepin fought for the pope against the Lombard king, Aistulf, and defeated the Lombards. Pepin then gave Aistulf's lands to the pope. The alliance between the Church and the Frankish kings became even stronger and more important under Pepin's son, Charlemagne.

By the middle of the eighth century, the Carolingian ruler, Pepin the Short, a son of Charles Martel, felt that it was time that he be formally recognized as the anointed king of the Franks in place of the weak Merovingian ruler. In 751 a Frankish assembly proclaimed Pepin king, and in 754 Pope Stephen II anointed him as king of the Franks and Patrician of the Romans. This last title meant that he was the protector of the city of Rome.

Though Pepin the Short was the first of the Carolingians to be called king, he was the third by that name in his family to rule the Franks. Thus he is called Pepin III. His kingdom included what is now northern and central France. His son, Charlemagne, would expand this rule to other regions.

There were many good reasons for cooperation between the new Carolingian ruler and the papacy. Pepin III knew that the support of the papacy would make it easier for the Franks to accept him as their ruler. Pope Stephen II wanted help against the Lombard king, Aistulf. Pepin III invaded Italy twice and took the former Byzantine section of Italy away from the Lombard king. He gave this land to the pope in his famous grant called the Donation of Pepin. This large section of land stretched from Rome in the west to Ravenna on the east coast of the Italian peninsula. This area would later form what would be called the Papal States.

The Lombards still held their lands in Italy, but this situation changed when Pepin's son Charlemagne, which means Charles the Great, inherited full rule over the Franks. The pope accused the Lombard king, Desiderius, of failing to live up to the peace settlement made in the time of Pepin III. Charlemagne invaded Italy and defeated Desiderius in 774. The king was taken prisoner, and the jewels and armor belonging to him and his nobles became the property of Charlemagne.

Now Charlemagne controlled Italy from the Alps in the north to the area just south of Rome. He made himself king of the Lombards, and thus the rule of the Lombards in northern Italy came to an end.

30. Charlemagne went to Rome as a humble pilgrim shortly before Easter in 774.
Pope Hadrian I welcomed him with great honor, and the two men prayed together at St. Peter's tomb.
They promised to be loyal to each other.

To the people of Europe, the Roman empire of the past seemed like a golden age. Under the rule of Charlemagne, the ideal of empire would be reborn, but with a difference. Now the empire not only would be Roman but would be holy—that is, it would be Christian and be supported by the Church. We see signs of this in the cooperation between Charlemagne and the pope.

Shortly before Easter in 774, Charlemagne, who was already in central Italy, made a pilgrimage to Rome. He arrived there with a large following, as kings usually had, and Pope Hadrian I made hurried preparations for the unexpected visit.

About thirty miles away from Rome, Charlemagne was met by a delegation of Roman nobles bearing all their insignia of nobility. It was a welcome reserved for rulers. When Charlemagne was about a mile from Rome, he was greeted by a parade of soldiers and military officers. He received all the honors that had once been reserved for the Byzantine rulers of Italy on their visits to Rome.

Charlemagne got off his horse and proceeded on foot, as a person on pilgrimage would do. The pope and the clergy of Rome welcomed him in St. Peter's, and Charlemagne asked permission to enter the city and pray as a pilgrim in the churches of Rome. Charlemagne and Hadrian prayed together at the tomb of St. Peter and vowed mutual loyalty. Then Charlemagne went to his lodgings, choosing one of the pilgrim hostels near St. Peter's rather than the imperial palace on the Palatine hill, which the pope had offered him.

On Easter Sunday and the days following, Charlemagne took part in the solemn services held by the pope. On Easter Monday, prayers of praise and thanks for the strength and protection of the Franks were offered to God for the first time by the pope and the people of Rome.

31. Charlemagne had conquered northern Italy and had pledged friendship with the pope. As the most powerful ruler in the West, Charlemagne was very active in church affairs. Italy was a patchwork of many different regions: Charlemagne's territory in the north, some Byzantine territory in the south, a few Lombard duchies, and the Papal States, which were just forming.

Charlemagne renewed pledges made to popes by his father, perhaps even adding to them. But he had taken over northern Italy from the Lombards, and he did not give that territory to the pope. Nor did he hesitate to express his views about church matters, or to make it clear that he regarded himself as the dominant ruler in Europe. Papal problems were increased by the fact that Italy contained many groups of people and cities who clung to their independence in thought, custom, and government.

Some Lombard duchies in Italy had not submitted to the Franks, and they continued to fight a long time for their independence. Sections of Italy that had been under the rule of the Byzantine emperor were still Greek Christian in outlook. At Ravenna, in particular, the culture was Greek and church life followed the thinking and practice of the eastern Church. In southern Italy, the Byzantine emperor still held lands and islands, Syracuse being the chief city. There the language and church organization was Greek, and many eastern monks were working to convert the area to Christianity.

Italy, then, was a patchwork of differing regions and interests. Charlemagne ruled northern Italy. The Byzantine emperor held territory in the south, and a few Lombard duchies lingered on. Slowly, the Papal States, ruled by the pope, were becoming a reality. Popes began to coin money of their own and to date years on the basis of their pontificates, or terms of office. They began to act as independent rulers, though they still tried to maintain ties with the emperor in Constantinople.

32. Charlemagne made war
on the Saxons
and conquered them
after many fierce battles.
He killed the Saxons
who would not be baptized.
At last the leader
of the Saxons agreed
to become Christian,
and peace came to the land.

Although the Franks had been subject to oman influence for centuries, they remained a Germanic people. Indeed, the Carolingian Franks may have been more hostile to Roman ways than the Merovingian Franks had been. In any case, the influence of Roman classical culture was little more than a dim memory for most people by this time.

The kingdom of the Franks, now ruled by Charlemagne, included parts of what is now France and parts of what is now Germany. It had been built up ever since the time of Clovis, and Charles Martel had managed to recover some lands that the descendants of Clovis had lost. Charlemagne would extend Christian Frankish boundaries even further, but this advance would halt around 804.

Directly to the north of the Frankish domains of Austrasia and Thuringia lay the territory of the Saxons, another Germanic people who had remained pagans. The Franks had tried many times to conquer them, but in vain; and so they had constructed many forts along the frontier between themselves and the Saxons. Christian missionaries, such as Willibrord and Boniface, had tried to preach the Gospel to the Saxons; and churches and monasteries also arose on the frontiers.

Charlemagne was eager to bring the territory of the Saxons, called Saxony, under his own political rule. Various Frankish expeditions advanced into Saxony, destroying fortresses and capturing hostages. At the Diet (or public assembly) of Paderborn in 777,

the Saxons submitted to Charlemagne and pledged their loyalty. But one Saxon group, under the leadership of a nobleman named Wittekind, was opposed to Frankish rule. This group started a major rebellion, to which Charlemagne responded ferociously. He organized a military expedition that pushed through Saxony as far as the Elbe River.

To make sure that his control would last this time, Charlemagne put nobles favorable to the Franks in charge of Saxony. He also decided that the Saxons had to become Christians, whether they liked it or not. But many Saxons preferred to remain faithful to their tribal paganism. It is said that 4,500 or more were put to death by the forces of Charlemagne for refusing to be baptized.

This slaughter is a sad story for Christians. Charlemagne was not wise enough to realize that the decision to become a Christian must be freely made. Even some close supporters of Charlemagne criticized him severely for this action. But when the Saxons broke out in a new revolt, Charlemagne used the same cruel force to put it down.

Finally, however, Charlemagne granted Wittekind a promise that he could come to meet with him in safety. He managed to convince Wittekind to become a Christian, and he himself acted as his godfather. Peace was restored, and Charlemagne ordered prayers of thanksgiving to be offered throughout his kingdom.

33. Charlemagne now turned his attention to the land we know today as Spain, which was ruled by the Muslims. Charlemagne took his army to Spain, intending to conquer it. He was defeated, and as his army retreated, the last troops were ambushed. Most of the soldiers were killed. This event is told in a famous epic poem, *The Song of Roland.*

Most of Spain had come under Muslim rule in the first part of the eighth century. A Muslim Berber army from north Africa had crossed the Strait of Gibraltar into Spain in 711 and defeated the Visigothic king, Roderick. The Muslim Berbers, usually known as the Moors, soon conquered most of the peninsula and set up their capital at Córdoba.

Many of the native Christians in Spain converted readily to Islam, while others tried to remain loyal to Christianity and to the Christian archbishop of Toledo. The Christians were allowed to retain their faith and their religious life. They had their own rulers, called counts, and their own clergy. But they had to pay certain taxes, which were collected by special agents. These Spanish Christians who lived in Muslim Spain but followed the Christian practices of earlier Visigothic Spain came to be called Mozarabs. Many of them probably spoke Arabic. Greatly influenced by Muslim culture, they in turn would exert great influence on later Spanish culture.

The disputes between Muslims in Spain, as well as the pleas of many Spanish Christians, made Charlemagne decide to try to win the country back to Christianity and place the region under his own rule. He crossed the Pyrenees mountains into Spain in 778. At first his army was successful, but it soon met strong resistance. Charlemagne decided to

give up his venture and head home. As Charlemagne's soldiers retreated, the troops of his rear guard—commanded by a nobleman named Roland—followed to protect them from attack. But as the rear guard went through the mountain pass of Roncevalles, they were ambushed by a band of mainly Christian Basques. The Franks suffered a heavy defeat. Among those killed was Roland.

French legends would soon begin to glorify the story of Roland. The whole incident has come down to us through the famous *Song of Roland*, which was put together in its present form during the eleventh or twelfth century. The Spanish, too, would tell their side of the story, recounting the glorious deeds of the Basque leader, Bernan del Carpio.

Charlemagne made no more attempts to conquer Spain, but he did continue to occupy an area of northern Spain. And he began to organize a defense against Moorish invasions of his territory. As time went on, more and more contacts would be made with small groups of Christians in northern Spain who were strongly opposed to Muslim rule.

34. The Franks extended their power, taking over Bavaria and defeating the Avars. The Avar king was baptized a Christian, and Charlemagne was his godfather. Now Charlemagne and his former enemy were now bound together in friendship.

Somewhat southeast of the Frankish kingdom, in the valley of the Danube River, lay the important and rich duchy of Bavaria. Boniface had brought Christianity there already. Church life centered around the diocese of Salzburg, which also was in charge of missionary work among Germanic and Slavic peoples who had not yet converted to Christianity.

The Bavarians were a fierce and proud people. They held to their old laws and obeyed their own dukes. They did not want to submit to Frankish rule. In 772 their duke was Tassilo. He was a strong defender of Bavarian independence, and he gave a new Christian duke to the people of one of his territories and persuaded them to accept new missionaries.

But Charlemagne wanted Bavaria to be under his rule. He made this intention clear to Tassilo, who appealed to Pope Hadrian I for support against Charlemagne. Charlemagne's representatives reminded Tassilo that the Bavarians had made a pledge of loyalty to Charlemagne's father, Pepin III. Tassilo refused to give in, and so Charlemagne's forces invaded his country. The defeated Tassilo was forced to retire to a monastery.

Once they were in control of Bavaria, the Franks found themselves confronting an even more threatening people—the Avars. These people were raiding nomads from central Asia who had made their way into the Hungarian plain. There they found good pasture land for their horses. For some time they had been a power in Europe, terrorizing the Slavs and even frightening the Lombards, who were supposed to be their allies.

Under Charlemagne's command the Franks attacked the Avars in force. Three Frankish armies fought against them, suffering much hardship. Finally the Franks overcame the Avars. At Aachen their leader surrendered and agreed to be baptized. Charlemagne was his godfather.

By becoming the godfather of the Avar king, Charlemagne showed that he accepted the king into his community or family. Now Charlemagne and the Avar king were no longer enemies. Instead, as godfather and godson, they were bound to each other by special ties of privilege and friendship.

35. Charlemagne was a strong military leader, but he also wanted to organize good government in his lands. He held meetings with learned people from his country to talk over problems, and then he wrote decrees or laws to settle the difficulties. Charlemagne wanted to establish just laws that would protect people.

Charlemagne certainly saw himself as a military leader. But he knew that conquest by war must be followed by good government. So Charlemagne was very active in organizing his government and passing laws. For this purpose he used capitularies—written decrees describing or ordering what should be done.

Every year, Charlemagne held a meeting with his chief advisers in some town of his realm. His advisers included counts, other local lords, bishops, and abbots. At the meetings, they discussed all aspects of life in his kingdom, including civil and church matters. Then, with the help of these advisers and legal experts, Charlemagne drew up general laws for his kingdom and decrees to settle particular problems. Then envoys of the king, who came to be known as *missi dominici,* were sent out as inspectors to make sure that the laws were obeyed. These envoys—who might be laymen or churchmen— also heard complaints from the people about local rulers or unfair practices. Usually at least two such envoys were sent out to work

in a given territory. This system of inspection and investigation was certainly a good idea and must have helped, but we cannot be sure that it worked as well in practice as it did on paper.

One of the most famous sets of capitularies was drawn up in 779 at the assembly that took place in Herstal—a town in what is now Belgium. One of these capitularies forbade the Germanic custom in which someone who had been offended or injured could take personal revenge on the offending party. Charlemagne's capitulary restored the old principle of Roman law, which gave the state the authority to punish wrongdoing. This helped to prevent injuries and murders by private citizens.

To ensure that qualified people would decide questions of law, and to prevent abuses of the law, another capitulary of Herstal decreed that judges should be selected fairly and that they should hold their office for life. This was meant to ensure that laws would work well and that people would respect them.

36. Though he was a smart man, Charlemagne was not well educated. But he valued learning, and he chose educated people for advisers and officials. Charlemagne organized a famous school in his palace where many subjects could be studied. This led to a rebirth of culture and learning called the Carolingian Renaissance.

Respected by his followers for his military deeds and leadership, Charlemagne had a broader vision than many of them. Though his own education was limited, he had a keen mind. Just as he saw the need for good laws and obedience to them, so he realized that sound learning and education would foster the spiritual growth of his kingdom. In 781 he asked Alcuin, a learned and pious English monk, to come and take charge of this work of reform and education. Alcuin accepted. He was the most influential person behind the revival of learning known as the Carolingian Renaissance.

Charlemagne welcomed learned men to his court. They helped him to make good decisions, and they taught in his palace school. The students of this school were sons of noblemen and other important people. When grown up, these students would become officials in the Frankish kingdom. Their experiences at the palace school would help them prepare for their work. At the school, they met and studied with many learned people: Alcuin, who had been head of the episcopal school and library at York; Dungal, an Irish monk noted for his knowledge of astronomy; and Paul the Deacon, an Italian from Lombardy who wrote a famous history of the Lombard reign in Italy. The palace school became famous, and it was a real center of education.

Alcuin convinced Charlemagne that he should make important reforms. He urged the emperor to divide his kingdom into church provinces. Each province was made up of several towns and dioceses under the authority of an archbishop or metropolitan. To enter into his office, the archbishop would have to receive the pallium—a band of woolen cloth worn around the neck. Only the pope could grant the pallium, and so every archbishop had to go to Rome and pledge his obedience to the pope. This helped to strengthen ties between the Frankish kingdom and the papacy, though Charlemagne had much say about who was nominated as a bishop.

Alcuin, as the head of the palace school, had a profound influence on the program of studies there. He thought that students should be taught how to study and understand the sacred Scriptures. But he also felt that students would learn how to write better if they studied ancient authors and thinkers such as Virgil and Horace. Writing, he felt, should be clear and simple. The Carolingian form of writing letters of the alphabet became common in much of Europe, and the small letters we use today come down to us from Charlemagne's school. Thus a whole system of education, which had been used to some extent in British monastery schools, spread through Europe. This revival of learning has been called the Carolingian Renaissance, or renewal.

37. Parish schools in towns
and villages began
to model themselves
after Charlemagne's famous
palace school. The parish
schools were improved, and
more schools were set up.
Charlemagne ordered that
the students learn
to read and write
in the common language
of the people instead
of only in Latin, the
language of educated people.

Charlemagne's palace school sparked a revival of learning throughout his kingdom. And since secular learning was associated with religious learning in those days, it was assumed that students would study the Gospel message and the truths of faith as well as such subjects as grammar, arithmetic, music, and astronomy. Schools, then, were centers of religious and spiritual life as well as secular teaching.

Charlemagne gave new life to schools associated with local parishes. Such schools had existed for a hundred years or more. There children and older people learned the basics of reading, writing, and arithmetic. They also learned the most important Christian prayers, the duties they had as Christians,

the use of the sacraments, and other basic truths of their faith. Charlemagne issued decrees and instructions stressing the need for such learning. He insisted that the students be taught in the common spoken language of the people rather than in Latin.

Charlemagne was also very concerned about local churches. He wanted them to train people in the faith and to adhere strictly to the practices of the Roman Church. He introduced into his kingdom the calendar of saints followed in Rome. More exact texts of writings by the Church Fathers were provided, and Rome's instructions on religious ceremonies and rites were made official in his kingdom. Finally, the rule of St. Benedict, which was followed in the monastery of Monte Cassino, became the model for all monasteries in Charlemagne's kingdom.

Thus the various church-related schools now had better tools for teaching and learning, and they could benefit from the use of people's ordinary language. The oldest examples we have of Old High German, the ancestor of the modern German language, come from this period of cultural revival under Charlemagne. The use of ordinary language in education may have helped the people of that time to realize that their spoken language had dignity and importance, even if it was not Latin. Such a realization would be an important step in cultural development.

38. Charlemagne was now the most powerful person in western Europe. He could enforce his ideas on almost anything— education, religion, division of lands. Many people thought he was as powerful as the emperor in Constantinople, the caliph in Baghdad, and the pope in Rome. In the year 800, Pope Leo III recognized Charlemagne's power and crowned him emperor of the Romans.

By the last decade of the eighth century, Charlemagne was the dominant figure in western Europe. He had won battles, had reorganized education and church life, and had stepped in to enforce his views about every sort of matter. Those around him praised him as the anointed of the Lord, suggesting that he was at least as important as the caliph in Baghdad, the emperor in Constantinople, and the pope in Rome. Indeed, when compared to other figures, Charlemagne always seemed to be the best of them all.

In 794 Charlemagne moved his capital from Herstal to Aachen, which was located nearer to the center of his kingdom. His actions there, in both politics and religion, strongly indicated that he saw himself as at least the equal of the emperor in Constantinople and the pope.

In 795, Leo III became pope, with the support of the Franks. Four years later, members of the Roman nobility charged Leo with many crimes and tried to remove him as pope. Very likely, these nobles acted with the

approval of the imperial government in Constantinople. Pope Leo III was taken prisoner, but he escaped and went to Charlemagne for help. Charlemagne gave the pope a troop of soldiers and officials, who took him safely back to Rome. The next year, Charlemagne himself went to Rome, investigated the charges against the pope, and declared that the pope was not guilty.

A few days later, on Christmas day in the year 800, Charlemagne went to St. Peter's to be present when the pope celebrated Mass. During Mass, the pope placed a golden crown on Charlemagne's head as Charlemagne knelt in prayer and proclaimed him, "Charles, the august, crowned by God, great and pacific emperor of the Romans." The pope then anointed Charlemagne with oil, just as the prophets had done in the Old Testament when they crowned the kings of Israel. Then the pope knelt before Charlemagne, the emperor.

The coronation of Charlemagne by the pope was a very important event, and it challenged the power of the emperor in Constantinople. Western Europe seemed to be claiming some independence from the old system of imperial government in which there was only one emperor over all nations of the world. For centuries afterward, many people interested in government emphasized the idea of a Holy Roman Emperor who would rule Europe with the approval of western religious authorities. This idea would cause many arguments, but no one seemed to doubt the reality of it.

39. Charlemagne's coronation
    as emperor angered the
    rulers in Constantinople.
    They felt that Charlemagne
    had taken some of the power
    and glory that belonged
    to the Byzantine emperor.
    For a time it seemed that
    war might break out
    between the Franks and
    the Byzantine empire.
    But a peaceful settlement
    was worked out. Then
    Charlemagne made plans
    to pass his empire on to
    his son Louis.

Charlemagne wanted to keep peace with the imperial authorities in Constantinople. At the time, the empress Irene ruled in the East. Charlemagne proposed marriage to her as a way of restoring unity in the Christian world. This proposal failed because in 802 Irene was deposed and replaced by the emperor Nicephorus I. Negotiations grew more difficult, and the two sides even engaged in battles for the coast around Venice. Finally, in 812, a settlement was reached. Charlemagne gave back Venice and other territory he had won. He also agreed not to try to capture more land in southern Italy. In return, the Byzantines agreed to let Charlemagne have the title of emperor, though they did not say what exactly he was emperor of. They referred to a western empire, but not to a Roman empire. The papacy, meanwhile, did not play any role in this settlement.

Charlemagne now began to take the title of emperor seriously for the first time. The next year, in 813, he crowned his own son Louis as his imperial successor in Aachen, with the approval of the Frankish nobility. A western empire now existed, it seemed, but it was to be ruled and passed on by the leader of the Franks. Only gradually would the notion of a Christian empire in the West take hold of people's minds as a major force for religious and civil unity.

40. Charlemagne died on January 22, 814. His son Louis became the emperor. We call him Louis the Pious. Louis was not a great leader, as Charlemagne had been, but he was deeply and sincerely interested in the welfare of the Church.

In 806 Charlemagne willed that his lands be divided among his three sons after his death. But two of them died, and so in 813 he willed his lands and his imperial title to his surviving son, Louis. On January 22, 814, Charlemagne died and Louis came to the Frankish throne in his place. The new emperor came to be known as Louis the Pious.

Louis was well educated for a person of his day, and his moral conduct was far better than his father's had been. Right from the start, he seems to have taken the title of emperor more seriously than Charlemagne did. And he sought helpers who would carry out his views, even if these views conflicted with older Frankish customs and practices.

Louis began at once to try to bring greater discipline into court life and the functions of government. Thoughtful and religious, Louis relied on a close circle of helpers to keep him in touch with other noblemen in his kingdom. Two or three times a year he would hold official assemblies, whereas Charlemagne had held them only once a year. But there were disputes with some groups of the Frankish nobility, and it was becoming difficult to maintain control over such vast territories. Moreover, outside threats were increasing once again. Louis would not be remembered in history as a ruler who had successfully met the challenges he had to face.

But his interest and involvement in the life of the Frankish Church was strong and genuine. In 816 a major reform council was held in Aachen, and it made important decisions for the Frankish Church. Monks were more clearly set apart from priests and lay people, and they were ordered to live in their monasteries under the rule of St. Benedict. Only rarely were monks to have visits from lay people, and monastic schools were to be only for monks or other people who intended to live according to the monastic spirit. Priestly life was also regulated. Priests were to live in small communities, reciting prayer together, maintaining schools, and assisting the faithful.

Louis maintained good relations with the pope, who crowned him as emperor in 816. He was deeply interested in the welfare of the Church, but it should be noted that the life and organization of the Frankish Church was very much, perhaps too much, under the control of Frankish rulers and Frankish noblemen. Because the rulers and noblemen had so much to do with the appointment of bishops, abbots, and other church officers, these churchmen tended to obey the Frankish nobility and to defend its position on all sorts of matters. But this wasn't always obvious when Frankish rulers and popes were on good terms with each other.

41. Louis the Pious asked Benedict of Aniane to become his adviser. Under Benedict's guidance, the Benedictine rule became the rule followed in all Frankish monasteries.

Important reforms in the Church took place during the lifetime of Louis the Pious, as we have already noted. In particular, the lifestyle and discipline of monks were reexamined and changed.

The great figure behind monastic reform was a Visigothic nobleman, whose original name was Witiza. He was born in 751 into a family allied with the Franks, and he began his studies at the court of one of Charlemagne's sons. He was a brave warrior, and he proved to be a heroic soldier when the Franks attacked Pavia. But Witiza began to realize that he was not meant to live as a court nobleman or as a military leader. In 780 he decided to become a monk in a monastery near Dijon. There he changed his name to Benedict, out of love and respect for the founder of the Benedictine Order.

The new monk soon made a name for himself in the monastery because he took the monastic life seriously and devoted himself eagerly to his studies. Benedict was especially interested in the rules governing the lives of monks. Many differing rules of monastic life were followed at the time, but

Benedict became convinced that the rule of St. Benedict was the best for helping monks to live their vocation properly. He decided to make sure that the Benedictine rule was properly obeyed in his monastery. Other practices and traditions that did not agree with the Benedictine rule were to be set aside or eliminated. But Benedict soon discovered that many monks preferred to live an easy, comfortable life rather than obey strict rules.

Benedict did not give up. Leaving the monastery near Dijon, he persuaded his father to give him a fairly large piece of land near Aniane. There Benedict built a monastery, and he and a few companions began to follow the Benedictine rule in all its strictness. Their example soon made a deep impression on other people. These monks spent the day praying, studying, and working. Unlike monks in other monasteries, they lived apart from the world and received few visitors or guests. People who were deeply interested in holiness went to Aniane to follow the example of Benedict. Many lords and bishops asked Benedict of Aniane to reform their local monasteries in a similar way.

When Louis the Pious became emperor, he asked Benedict to serve as his adviser. Benedict had much to do with Louis's reform of church and monastery life. Even in the year 811, before Charlemagne's death, a council in Aachen had decided that the rule of St. Benedict must be followed in all Frankish monasteries. Thus Benedict of Aniane can be considered the second founder of Benedictine monasticism, since he did much to restore it to the ideals of the first St. Benedict.

**42. The Carolingian Renaissance continued, and new centers of education and culture arose during the reign of Louis the Pious.
They included centers in Lyons, where there was a famous cathedral school, and in the abbey of Fulda, which had been founded by St. Boniface.**

The Carolingian Renaissance was a cultural movement that arose in the court of Charlemagne, first in Herstal and then in Aachen. The Renaissance continued during the reign of Charlemagne's son, Louis the Pious. Louis favored religious literature above all else. He dismissed poets and other sorts of writers from his court because he felt that such writing was not serious enough. This made his court school smaller, but educational and cultural activity did not grow less. The artists and writers now lived at courts of other noblemen throughout the Frankish kingdom, thus giving rise to new centers of culture.

The most famous of these new centers was in the town of Lyons, in Burgundy. In Lyons there was a famous cathedral school—a school run by priests near the cathedral church. Future priests and smart youngsters were able to study at this school. The location of Lyons made it a cultural meeting place for the people of southern Europe. Spain and Italy, for example, sent many students and teachers to the school in Lyons.

The director of the school in Lyons was Agobard, one of Louis's most trusted advisers. With his disciple Florus, Agobard worked hard to reduce the influence of lay lords on church life. This was a problem, because many lay lords had founded their own churches and monasteries. They felt that this gave them the right to set rules for the priests and monks in these churches and monasteries. Agobard disagreed, saying that gifts of land or money did not give the donors any rights to run the Church. Gifts should be given, he said, for unselfish reasons.

Agobard and Florus also examined the prayers used by priests, taking out statements or ideas that were not a part of true Christian tradition. Another member of Agobard's school, Maximus of Turin, was known for his opinion on the use of religious images. Like some eastern Christians, he was against their use.

Another great center of culture in the days of Louis the Pious was the abbey of Fulda, which had been founded by St. Boniface. Its most famous scholar was Rabanus Maurus, who was originally from Mainz. Rabanus had studied under Alcuin, and he was considered the best expert on Christian literature in his day. He was also a fine school administrator. Rabanus did much to spread the work of the Carolingian Renaissance. His works were read throughout Germany, and he came to be known as the "teacher of Germany." Whereas scholars usually wrote in Latin, Rabanus began to write in German, the spoken language of the people. The word *German* was first employed by Rabanus and some of his followers.

43. Wala, one of Charlemagne's brave warriors, was forced by Louis the Pious to leave the royal court. Wala became a monk.
Louis then called him back to court to help govern the lands. Wala tried to stop the quarreling in the empire, and he also tried to help the Church be more free of the king.

Around 825 the empire faced new wars. Even more of a problem, however, were the disputes and the signs of bad government within the empire itself. One man who spoke out against these problems was Wala of Corbie, an upholder of the old imperial ideal.

Wala and his brother Adalard came from a Carolingian royal family and were relatives of Charlemagne and Louis the Pious. The two brothers served the empire courageously and loyally during the life of Charlemagne. After his death, however, they were forced to leave the emperor's court because of their disagreement with Louis the Pious. Withdrawing to the monastery of Corbie, they thought about the empire and the best way to govern it.

It was not long before they were missed at court. In 821 Louis the Pious publicly admitted that he had made a mistake in driving them away. He asked them to return and help him once again in governing the empire. Adalard became one of Louis's advisers, and Wala became an adviser to Louis's son, Lothair. In 826 Adalard died. Only Wala remained as an upholder of the older imperial ideal that had made the Carolingian house great.

In 828 an assembly was held in Aachen to put an end to disorders in the empire. For that assembly, Wala wrote a statement or report in which he severely criticized Louis, Lothair, and the whole court. He urged the emperor and his son to be more serious about governing, and he asked them to punish those noblemen who were seeking only their own interests. Those who rule, said Wala, should try to do what is good for the empire and the Church; they should not think only about themselves. Moreover, said Wala, the emperor and his nobles should not try to claim rights over the property of the Church, much less give orders to churchmen. The empire and the Church are two different living things, and they should remain distinct. The empire should promote civil peace and social life; the Church should concern itself with the welfare of souls. Noblemen and rulers should leave the Church alone. In return, bishops, abbots, and priests should concentrate on their spiritual tasks and leave the government of the empire to its rulers.

Wala's statement could be seen as the last will and testament of that old knight and nobleman. It made an impression on those who heard it. If heeded, it might have done much to maintain peace and order in the empire.

44. Louis the Pious divided his empire between his three older sons. Later, Louis wanted to take back some of the land and give it to his son Charles, the youngest of the four. Refusing to give up any land, the three older sons made war against their own father. Louis the Pious was defeated.

One problem in Carolingian government was the question of succession to the imperial throne. The Frankish emperors tended to look on the empire as their personal property, which was to be divided up among their sons. In 806 Charlemagne himself had divided his kingdom among his three sons. But two of them died soon after, and so Louis the Pious had inherited the whole kingdom.

The problem became much more serious for Louis the Pious. First he divided his kingdom up among his three older sons: Lothair, Pepin, and Louis the German. Later he tried to alter this division, because he wanted to give some territory to Charles, his younger son by a second marriage. But his

other sons opposed this idea, as did the old adviser Wala. The sons wanted to keep the land they had been given; and Wala pointed out that the idea of the empire as the emperor's personal property could only make survival of the empire more difficult.

In 830 Lothair led a revolt against Louis the Pious and forced his father to let the three older sons keep their lands. But fighting and disagreement between those who had revolted enabled Louis the Pious to gain the upper hand again. Once more he decided to divide up the empire in a new way, so that Charles would have a share.

And once again the sons of Louis the Pious marched against their father. The eldest son,

Lothair, who had inherited Italy, even asked Pope Gregory IV to step in as a peacemaker between the two sides. In a message to the emperor, Pope Gregory IV reminded Louis that though he was the ruler, he was also in the service of the empire, and so he could not dispose of its lands in any way he felt like doing. The pope also reminded the sons that they had a duty to respect their father.

These efforts to make peace failed. Open warfare followed and on June 24, 833, the army of Louis's sons defeated the army of their father once again. Louis the Pious was forced to enter a monastery.

45. The empire was in confusion after the defeat of Louis the Pious. Wala tried to make peace, but he was now tired and old.
He died in 836. Louis and one of his sons were killed in battles, and in 843 the empire was divided into three kingdoms.

After his defeat in 833, Louis the Pious was forced to live in a monastery. In reality he was almost kept a prisoner by his son Lothair. But as time passed, the public grew angry about the fate of Louis. Many people wanted him to regain his freedom and a position of honor.

Again Wala raised his voice in protest over the situation. He went to see the eldest son, Lothair, and helped to convince him that he should free his father. But Wala was not fully satisfied when Louis was released. He wanted real peace and harmony between father and son for the sake of the empire. Compromise would lead only to another war at some point, he felt.

SACRVM ROMANVM IMPERIVM a.Ọ. 843

■ Charles's Kingdom
□ Lothair's Kingdom
◨ Louis's Kingdom

But Wala's energies were used up. In 836 he died, probably sad to see the decline of the imperial ideal that he had tried to serve loyally and unselfishly. He wanted a united Christian empire that would give order and encouragement to the Christian way of life. Just as the Church looked out for the welfare of souls, so the empire should provide good government for the social welfare of its citizens. For all his faults, Charlemagne had shown that this was possible. His example remained firmly imprinted on Wala's mind. But selfish interests had gained the upper hand, and the sons of Louis the Pious put an end to Wala's vision.

The death of Wala might also be considered the end of the great imperial ideal. There were more battles, and in the course of time both Louis the Pious and his son Pepin died. Finally, in 843, a treaty was signed at Verdun by the three remaining sons of Louis

the Pious: Lothair, Louis the German, and Charles the Bald.

Louis got an eastern kingdom in the region we now call Germany. Charles, the youngest son, got a western kingdom, which is now mainly France. Lothair, the eldest son, got a middle kingdom between the two. It stretched diagonally from the northwest to the southeast, including Friesland, Lorraine, Burgundy, Provence, and that part of Italy ruled by the Franks.

The treaty brought peace, but it marked the first stage in the breakup of the Carolingian empire. Over the course of time, the middle kingdom of Lothair would disappear. Broken into various fragments, most of it would be divided between the countries we know today as France, Germany, and Italy. A new Europe—a second Europe—was beginning to emerge from the ruins of Charlemagne's first Europe.

46. During this time, Spain was under Muslim rule. The caliph of Córdoba was the ruler. A lively culture developed, as Jews, Christians, and Muslims lived side by side. But in northern Spain, Christian people made plans to take Spain back from the Muslims.

In 756, Muslims, Jews, and Christians lived side by side, in Córdoba, Spain, under the rule of the Muslim caliph. A strong, lively culture developed.

Many Jews had found their way to Spain. They were farmers, doctors, businessmen, traders, administrators, philosophers, and scholars. Some of the most important works of medieval Jewish culture were composed in Spain.

There were many Christians, of course. They were allowed to have their own churches and practice their religion. These Christians, known as Mozarabs, lived on fairly equal terms with everyone else for the

most part. Some of them were officials and administrators.

Córdoba became a great center of culture, perhaps the finest in Europe for hundreds of years. Its splendid mosque introduced a new way of building, which was copied in other parts of the Muslim world. The great library in Córdoba was a major center for theological, legal, and scientific studies. Great philosophers, such as Ibn Massarra, and great doctors, such as Zabrawl, were teachers there. New and original ideas in many fields were passed on to other countries in Europe: how to farm the land, how to dress and cook, and how to write poetry and literature.

Meanwhile, one small kingdom in the north of Spain had remained free of the Muslims. This was the kingdom of Asturias. The people of Asturias were loyal to the Franks, their friends and protectors. The Franks had too many problems of their own to try to free Spain from Muslim rule; and so the rulers of Asturias undertook the task of gradually reconquering Spain from the Muslims. This was a long, hard job, and it took many centuries. As the reconquest went on, the victorious Christians began to replace existing forms of civil and church life with those used by the Franks and by the papacy.

47. In the ninth century,
the island of Sicily,
which had been part
of the Byzantine empire,
fell to the Muslims.
For several centuries
after this conquest,
the Muslims and Christians
of Sicily joined
to create a rich culture.

In the early ninth century, the coastal areas of Africa around the city of Tunis were an important center of Muslim activity. Military actions and naval raids were launched from there against Egypt and the whole central area of the Mediterranean Sea. The Muslim raiders were often called Saracens, though this name should be given only to the people of northwest Arabia.

One island in the Mediterranean Sea was particularly important—Sicily. This island was under the rule of the Byzantine emperor, but it was fairly close to Tunis by sea. Southern Italy, including Rome, was also fairly close to Tunis. This region offered rich plunder to those who could take it.

In 827 the Muslims began to send out military expeditions to Sicily and Italy. It took them almost half a century to capture Sicily, but they finally succeeded. Palermo fell to them first, then Syracuse, the Byzantine capital in Sicily, and finally Taormina.

After taking over Sicily, the Muslims turned it into one of the major Muslim centers in the Mediterranean area. Under their rule, Sicily became rich and prosperous. Agriculture flourished, and many new products from the East were introduced, such as

rice, citrus trees, sugar cane, and date palms.

Sicily thus became a great commercial crossroad between the East and the West, between the Muslim world and the Christian world. There Christian merchants from the coastal towns of Italy, France, and Spain could meet Muslim merchants from Syria, Iraq, and Persia. Palermo, the new Muslim capital, was a magnificent city. No city in Christian Europe compared with it. Visitors admired the size and wonders of the city, whose mosques almost matched those of Córdoba.

Many different peoples intermingled in Palermo. There one could find Greeks, Lombards, Jews, Slavs, Berbers, Persians, Tartars, and black Africans. Peoples of many different races and faiths coexisted peacefully. This was the kind of coexistence that Islam had managed to accomplish in many different places.

Christians rarely suffered serious persecution. They clung to their religion, and they were allowed to live by their old laws for the most part. The local Christian clergy did not encourage movements of opposition or revolt. For many decades, Christians continued to live according to the customs of Byzantine culture, even though they also accepted part of the new world of Islam on their island. Sicily thus became an important place where the ideas and advances of Muslim culture and religion were passed on to the people of western Europe.

48. Around 850, the Vikings
began to make terrifying
raids on western Europe.
Three English kingdoms
fell to the raiders.
Under the leadership
of King Alfred the Great,
the fourth English kingdom
fought back successfully
against the Vikings.
King Alfred began a
revival of culture and
had important Christian

writings translated
into Anglo-Saxon,
the language of the people.

In the middle of the ninth century, England was made up of four kingdoms. Three of these kingdoms, however, fell under the terrifying attacks of raiders from the north of Europe. Those raiders were called the Danes, the Northmen, the Norsemen, and later, the Normans. We know them today as

the Vikings. For two centuries, they sailed along the coasts of Europe, making cruel attacks on the population and looting wherever they could. One group even went as far as northern Russia and settled there, giving the country the name it bears today. Throughout Christian Europe from the ninth to the eleventh centuries, people offered the following prayer: "From the fury of the Northmen, O Lord, deliver us."

Under the rule of King Alfred, one kingdom in England managed to fight off the Vikings: the kingdom of Wessex. The fight went on for ten years until Alfred managed to defeat King Guthrum, the Viking leader. Guthrum publicly acknowledged his defeat by agreeing to be baptized.

The fight against the pagan Vikings went on unsuccessfully for about fifty years in other parts of England. The Church was thrown into almost complete chaos. Cathedrals were burned down and monasteries were destroyed. Bishops, abbots, and monks wandered around the countryside, with no permanent place to live.

King Alfred, who came to be known as Alfred the Great, realized how serious the situation was, and he tried to do something about it. He summoned church leaders and officials to his court. One by one he appointed them to take charge of a diocese, or a monastery, or some church. Alfred the Great also tried to start a religious and cultural revival. He ordered important Christian writings, such as those of St. Augustine and Pope Gregory the Great, to be translated into the Anglo-Saxon language.

Alfred's work, however, did not have the great impact that Charlemagne's work had had earlier. England was in too much turmoil from the struggles with the Vikings to develop a big cultural revival at this time.

49. Cyril and Methodius brought the Christian message to the Slavs in eastern Europe. They were sent to Moravia by the emperor in 862. Cyril and Methodius used the Slavic language of the people in prayers and the liturgy.

The Slavs were one of the most numerous peoples living east of the Germans in Europe. Many Slavic tribes lived under the rule of the emperor in Constantinople, but others occupied independent principalities and duchies, including Moravia. These duchies were often in conflict with the eastern Franks ruled by Louis the German, for the Franks wanted control over the land occupied by the Slavs.

In 862, Rastislav, the duke of Moravia, asked the emperor in Constantinople to send some Christian missionaries. Two brothers, Cyril and Methodius, were particularly suited to carry out this task. Cyril had studied in Constantinople under the best teachers of the day, and he had become a deacon. He may also have been ordained a priest. In 860 he had been sent as a missionary and an ambassador to the Khazars, a Turkish people who ruled a kingdom that lay north of the Black Sea. The Khazars had a fairly high level of civilization and tolerated different religions in their region. In this territory, Cyril found what was believed to be the remains of St. Clement of Rome, who had died there in exile. Cyril's brother, Methodius, had been an imperial official before entering a monastery in Asia Minor and

eventually becoming its abbot. Both brothers knew the Slavic language well.

At the request of the emperor, Cyril and Methodius left Constantinople and headed for distant Slavic territory in the north. They were joyfully welcomed by the Moravians, and they set right to work educating and preaching to the people. They did not hesitate to use the language of the people, and they translated the Gospel and other Mass prayers into Slavic. Using Greek and Roman letters as their basis, they made a new alphabet, the glagolithic, to write down the Slavic language.

50. Cyril and Methodius were invited to Rome by the pope. There they were given a triumphant welcome. Cyril later died, and Methodius was consecrated a bishop. He returned to his missionary work, preaching to the Slavic tribes and organizing the Church in what is now Hungary and Bulgaria.

For three years the two brothers taught in the duchy of Rastislav. But they were not bishops, and so they could not ordain their young students to the priesthood. They decided to go back to Constantinople to try to resolve this problem, and they chose to sail from Venice. There, however, they had to defend their work before an assembly of bishops, priests, and monks, who accused them of using a language that was not approved for the liturgy. Then, suddenly, in 867, the pope invited them to Rome.

Cyril and Methodius readily accepted the pope's invitation to come to Rome. Pope Hadrian II and a crowd of Roman citizens met them on their arrival. Then they all went to the church of St. Clement, where Cyril placed the relics of St. Clement that he had brought with him.

But in Rome, too, there were monks and priests who criticized the two missionaries for using the Slavic language in the Mass. Many people felt that there were only three sacred languages: Latin, Greek, and Hebrew. These were the only three languages that had

been used for the words inscribed on the cross of Jesus.

Cyril and Methodius said that every people should be allowed to pray to God in their own language. The pope agreed with them, making it clear that he approved of their work. He let them celebrate their Slavic liturgy in the churches of Rome. He consecrated Methodius a bishop. And some of the young Slavs who had accompanied the two missionaries were ordained priests or deacons by the pope.

Cyril, who had done so much to spread Christianity and promote church unity, was very ill. On February 14, 869, he died in Rome and was buried in the basilica of St. Clement. His tomb is there to this very day. Methodius, with the pope's blessing, returned to his mission land.

Things had changed in Moravia, however. The Franks had deposed the old duke, Rastislav, who had supported Methodius and his work. So Methodius set out for the region around Lake Balaton in Pannonia, which is part of Hungary today. At this time, the territory was occupied by the Slovenes, a Slavic people. The Hungarian people of today, the Magyars, had not yet moved into this area.

The pope wanted to make it easier for Methodius to convert these people under the direct supervision of Rome rather than under the control of the Franks. So he created a large new metropolitan see at Sirmium, which is near the present-day city of Belgrade in Yugoslavia. Methodius became the archbishop of Sirmium. He was responsible for preaching the Gospel and building up the Church in a huge region occupied by many different Slavic tribes. The church province included the northern Balkans, the plains of Pannonia, and territory reaching as far as Moravia. For a short time, the people of this whole region would be able to share a common Christian way of life.

51. The Frankish rulers and some bishops opposed Methodius because they wanted to control the lands over which he was bishop. Methodius was put into prison. After his release, he returned to Moravia.

Many people were not happy about the new authority of Methodius. The eastern Franks were annoyed because they wanted to have political control over the land and people in his archdiocese. And the bishops of Bavaria, who had been in charge of missionary work in those regions, thought they had a right to control the Church in Moravia, Pannonia, and the Balkans.

With the encouragement of the Franks, Methodius's enemies captured him and made him a prisoner. Then he was put on trial in Bavaria before a church synod in November, 870. The German bishops present treated him very harshly and accused him of being an intruder. They decided to put him out of the Church and to imprison him.

To support these charges, the archbishop of Salzburg wrote a long report on the foundation of his Church and its missionary activity. Methodius replied that it was the pope who had the right to assign dioceses and mission territories, but his words of self-defense were useless. He was taken to Swabia and imprisoned in a monastery, despite the protests of Pope Hadrian II. Methodius spent two and one-half years as a prisoner. Finally, a new pope, John VIII, managed to get him freed.

The Moravians had begged the pope to send Methodius back to them. When he returned, they welcomed him enthusiastically. Methodius continued to carry on his missionary work, to use the Slavic language in the liturgy and written works, to preach, and to baptize. He inspired young followers to grow in their faith, their love of learning, and their zeal for missionary work. Thanks to their work, Christianity would be preached in all Slavic territories. Three outstanding followers of Methodius were Gorazd, Clement, and Naum.

In 882 Methodius went to Constantinople, where he was warmly welcomed by the emperor and the patriarch. There, too, his missionary work and church activity were approved. Methodius spent his last years making sure that the main liturgical and religious books were translated into the Slavic language. His circle of learned followers would produce two fine books in defense of the Christian faith and the Slavic Church. One was a life of Cyril, which may have been written by Clement at the urging of Methodius. The other was a life of Methodius, written soon after his death on April 6, 885.

52. After Methodius's death,
his followers were treated
cruelly and unjustly.
Many of them were forced
to leave the country.
Naum and Clement, two
priests who were among
Methodius's best helpers,
went to the territory of
the Bulgars.

The death of the great archbishop Methodius had serious consequences for all the peoples under his care. The bishop of Nitra, a Swabian named Wiching, had been a long-standing rival of Methodius in Moravia. Nitra was the main fortress of the Franks living in Moravia. As soon as Methodius died, Wiching hurried to Rome to convince Pope Stephen V that Methodius had been disobedient. He also claimed that Methodius had taught heretical ideas about the Holy Spirit. The pope put Wiching in charge of the diocese of Moravia.

It was a difficult period for the followers of Methodius. The use of their Slavic language in the liturgy was forbidden, and they were treated very unjustly. Some priests were made slaves and sold in the slave market of Venice. The best followers of Methodius were imprisoned. Then, driven out of the country, they were stripped of their clothes and left on the bank of the Danube River.

One such group, which included Naum and Clement, made a long trip down the Danube River and reached the territory of the Bulgars. Their ruler, Boris I, had been baptized in 864; but most of the Bulgars were still pagans. Boris realized that he needed well-trained priests to spread Christianity in his territory, and that such priests would have to be able to speak the language of the people. The Bulgars had originally been a Turkish-speaking people, but they had gradually adopted the language of the Slavic people they had conquered in this region. So Boris I welcomed the fleeing followers of Methodius and gave them a chance to carry on the work of Cyril and Methodius in his kingdom.

Remembering the work of Methodius in Moravia, Clement organized a school where the best local youths could study and prepare for the priesthood. Some of them would do

further theological study and write books. Clement's work was very successful. Tradition claims that a few thousand young men were educated in only a few years. The school was located in Ohrid, in what is Yugoslavia today. Clement became the bishop of the region.

Clement's companion, Naum, was another great educator and preacher of Christianity. He worked in Preslav, to the north. When Clement became a bishop, Naum moved to the vicinity of Clement's school and continued to educate young people. He built the monastery of the Holy Archangels—which still exists there today—and became a monk in it. Soon after his death, the local people began to venerate him as a saint.

The Bulgars received much from these two men: Christian faith, an organized church, the Slavonic Liturgy, an educational system, and the first written works dealing with their own history.

The tradition of Cyril and Methodius also continued to live among the Croats in the central Balkans. Under such leaders as Domagoj and Tomislav, the Croats freed themselves from the rule of the Franks. Tomislav was elected their king in 925, and the Croats remained faithful to the Slavonic Liturgy for many years.

53. By the end of the ninth century, the Frankish emperors were weak, and the popes received little support from them. More and more, the popes were coming under the control of noble families in Rome.

When the emperor Louis II, son of Lothair, died in 875, a fierce dispute arose over who would be the next emperor. The pope, John VIII, was deeply and actively involved in these disputes. He was to be one of the last forceful popes for some time, and he saw that the relationship between emperor and pope was an important matter. But the Carolingian empire had by this time fallen apart. The emperor had lost his power to local counts and dukes. The Carolingian family would continue for a while, and there would be

Carolingian emperors, but the empire of Charlemagne no longer existed.

Troubles loomed ahead for the papacy also. Pope John VIII wanted to rule the territory of the Papal States without interference from the outside. He did not want to be overruled by powerful Frankish nobles in the empire. He was worried about defending Rome from the Muslims, who now controlled the Mediterranean. He had serious disputes with Constantinople. But he managed to solve only the last of these problems before he died.

The popes who came after John VIII were not able to control the Roman nobility. During the next twenty years, there were seven popes. Each time the "chair of St. Peter"—as the papacy was sometimes called—was empty, Frankish and Lombard lords and the nobles of old Roman families decided, often with bloodshed, who should be the next pope. This domination over the pope and Rome by influential families of Rome would continue for some time to come.

54. Though Europe had many problems, culture and literature continued to develop. New schools were built in Sens, Rheims, Mainz, and Salzburg. Bishops and abbots wrote books and taught.

Despite the problems in Europe, cultural activity and religious life continued to grow. The court of the emperor was not the great court it had been under Charlemagne, but there were now many small courts of nobles where learning, literature, and church activity were encouraged. These nobles liked to act independently, and each tried to make his court the best in some way.

These many new courts were still the courts of Christian noblemen, who knew about Charlemagne and his work. Education was closely tied to religious studies. Bishops and abbots were linked with these courts, and so were the large and important monasteries. Thus there were ties between the courts and the work going on in local churches.

The work of various bishops in their own dioceses was very important during this period. They used their authority and power to begin new centers of culture in such places as Sens, Rheims, Mainz, and Salzburg. Many bishops wrote books about the history of the Church and the lives of the saints. The urge to teach people and the desire to make sense of what was going on in human life had not disappeared.

55. Christians continued to study their faith, helped by such teachers and writers as John Scotus Erigena. The presence of Jesus in the Eucharist was one of the questions discussed— a mystery of faith thought and prayed about in every age.

Christians did not stop thinking about the whole drama of their faith during this period. Somewhere around 847, Charles the Bald asked an Irishman to take charge of his court school in Paris. This man's name has come down to us as John Scotus Erigena, which simply means John the Scot of Ireland.

It seems that Erigena was the most learned and probing mind in the Christian world of his day. He knew Greek, as did most Irish monks. But few monks in Europe did. At the request of Charles the Bald, Erigena

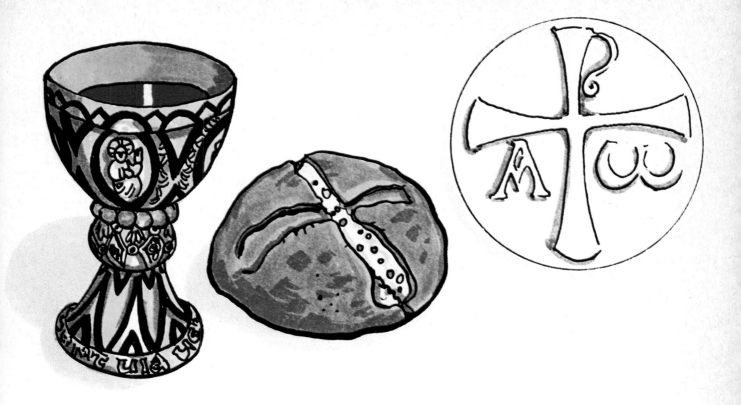

translated the writings of a person called
Pseudo-Dionysius—a person who had
claimed to be an Athenian converted to
Christianity by St. Paul himself. His claim
was not true, but his works remained an important heritage for Christians throughout
the Middle Ages. After translating this
writer's works, Erigena eventually wrote his
own major work. It was based on the idea of
all things beginning in God, moving on from
there, and returning to God in the end. That
basic idea is called Neoplatonism, and

Erigena is perhaps the most moving
representative of that idea in the medieval
Christian world.

At this time, there were also debates about
exactly how Jesus was present in the Eucharist, a mystery that Christians have prayer-
fully thought about in every age. During
Erigena's time, these discussions stayed
close to the faith taught by the Church, but in
the centuries to come, deep divisions would
come between Christians over this sacred
subject.

56. In the ninth century, Gottschalk, a Saxon monk, became convinced that people were destined at birth for heaven or hell.
This mistaken view was condemned by the Church, which taught that
God wanted each person to choose freely whether to accept God's offer of salvation.

Far more serious than the discussion about Jesus' presence in the Eucharist was another debate in the ninth century, which was started by a monk named Gottschalk. Gottschalk came from a Saxon noble family. While still a boy, he was placed in the monastery of Fulda. He may have been forced against his will to become a monk. In any case, he was freed from his vows around 829. Then he changed his mind, went to another monastery, and was ordained a priest. He traveled much, doing missionary work among the Croats and the Bulgars and also going on pilgrimages to Rome.

Gradually Gottschalk became convinced that the destiny of every human being was already decided at birth. In God's plan, according to Gottschalk, a person at the time of birth was already headed for salvation and heaven or for damnation and hell. Thus, Jesus came to save only those whom God had already chosen to be saved. This idea is known as predestination.

Gottschalk had discussed his views in several letters to his abbot. These views were submitted to a meeting of bishops for examination. It seemed quite clear that the idea of predestination went against the traditional teaching and experience of the Christian Church. Christians felt that God wanted human beings to respond freely to his offer of salvation. Being infinitely wise, God knew the secrets in people's hearts and the way they would decide, but the decision was up to them. Thus, Gottschalk's views were condemned by one meeting of bishops after another.

Gottschalk himself was stripped of his priestly functions and imprisoned in a monastery. Even though he had mistaken views, his religious concerns were deep and sincere. His thoughts on predestination made the whole Church give more serious thought to the gifts of free will and faith that God had given to human beings.

57. Toward the end of the ninth century, the Church established some new and better methods of organization. Archbishops gained more authority, and archdeacons became helpers of bishops.

As we saw earlier, Charlemagne passed laws to strengthen the religious and cultural life of local churches. The network of local churches was expanded, and they began to be organized into various dioceses. A diocese was a group of local churches or parishes in a certain region, and it was under the direction of a bishop.

Two functions became especially important in this period as aids for local bishops. One of them was that of the dean, a senior priest in a local area who offered advice to his bishop and kept watch over the lifestyle and work of priests in his area. The other function, a new one, was that of the archdeacon, who kept track of parish boundaries and parish administration.

Bishops continued to play an important role in the Church. Each bishop had his own territory, usually a walled-in town, and there he had his church, called a cathedral. Christians of the town were proud of their cathedral. They helped to build it and gave gifts of money and goods to make it more beautiful.

The bishop controlled farms and vineyards owned by the Church. And he had a big staff of people to help him run the diocese. Bishops had to do many of the things for the people that a good government does. They built schools, provided jobs, and took care of the sick and the poor. In times of want, they opened their storehouses and gave food to the people. Around that time, a saying began among the people: "It is good to live under the crosier." The crosier is the curved staff a bishop carries. It is a reminder of a shepherd's crook and recalls Christ's words to Peter: "Feed my sheep."

During this same period, archbishops began to play a more important role. Their office was higher than the bishops', and usually a number of bishops worked in the territory of one archbishop. When archbishops were appointed, they went to Rome to receive the pallium from the pope. This band of woolen cloth worn around the neck was a sign of the archbishops' high office and of the strong tie between the archbishops and the pope. The archbishops carried back to the bishops the decisions and plans of the pope. When questions came up that could not be settled by the bishops, the archbishops took these questions to Rome to discuss them with the pope. Also, the archbishops served as middlemen between the bishops and the civil rulers, since many civil laws also dealt with church matters.

58. Now that the Carolingian empire was no longer united and strong, it could not protect Christian kingdoms from attack. In the middle of the ninth century, Muslim raiders began to launch attacks on Italian villages and towns. In 882 they burned the great Benedictine abbey of Monte Cassino, an important center of learning and religious life.

When the Carolingian empire had been fairly united and well organized, it was able to discourage attacks on Christian lands in the West. But once the empire was weakened by inheritance disputes and the increased power of local nobles, the Muslims of Africa and Spain began to spread northward again. Spanish Muslims began to move into Provence, while African and Sicilian Muslims began to raid southern Italy regularly and loot its coastal towns. In places where they met little or no resistance in Italy, the Muslims dug trenches and set up armed camps for temporary housing and defense against attacks.

Weakened by internal fighting, the Frankish emperor was no longer in a position to defend papal territory. Only the Byzantines put up a courageous defense. The Muslims grew even bolder, threatening Rome itself. But perhaps the place that suffered most was the famous abbey of Monte Cassino.

Monte Cassino was built by St. Benedict, the man who did so much to organize monastic life in western Europe. In the seventh century, Monte Cassino began to symbolize the meeting of many new peoples in Italy, because Frankish and Lombard monks joined the monastery.

The abbey of Monte Cassino was admired by both Lombards and Franks. The rule of St. Benedict was strictly followed by the Benedictine monks who lived there. Charlemagne had asked them to send an accurate copy of their rule to his territory so that Frankish monasteries might follow it correctly. One of the more well-known monks of Monte Cassino, Paul the Deacon, was invited to Charlemagne's court to spread its learning in Frankish lands. At the emperor's court, Paul wrote a famous history of the Lombards.

Besides being a center of religious life and learning, the abbey of Monte Cassino was also a center of economic activity. The vast lands donated to the abbey were well farmed and administered. The monastery had grown, and new buildings had been added to it.

In 882, however, this great center was destroyed and burned by the Muslims. But it would rise again from the ashes to bear witness to the greatness and vitality of the rule of St. Benedict.

59. Though the pagan Vikings were feared for their cruel raids, the Church wanted to convert them.
A Frankish monk, Anskar, went to Denmark and southern Sweden to preach the Gospel. He set up small mission stations in the northern lands.

The northern part of western Europe—the area now known as Norway, Sweden, and Denmark—had never been occupied by the Romans. Only a few merchants and traders had made their way there to exchange Roman products with the Germanic tribes of the area. Christianity had not found its way there either. Then, in the ninth century, the Northmen of Europe suddenly stepped onto the stage of history as great sailors and explorers, superb ship builders, and savage raiders, striking terror into the other peoples of western Europe. The Northmen, or Vikings, were skilled at political organization in foreign lands as well. The period from the ninth to the eleventh centuries has often been called the Age of the Vikings.

In 825 Harold Klak, who claimed the right to the throne of Denmark, became a friend of the emperor Louis the Pious. He was converted to Christianity and baptized in Mainz. Louis gave him the county of Hriustri on the North Sea in return for Harold's pledge of loyalty. Then a Frankish monk, Anskar, was given the task of preaching Christianity in Harold's lands.

Harold failed to win the crown of Denmark and was driven out in 827. But Anskar returned to the area with some of his converts and was able to begin the real conversion of Denmark and southern Sweden. In 831 the diocese of Hamburg was set up in northern Germany to take charge of the mission to Scandinavia. Anskar himself settled in Bremen and continued to go out preaching in Denmark and Sweden.

Until his death in 865, Anskar continued to travel to the two countries, to preach the Gospel message, and to leave behind faithful followers who would carry on his work. Small mission stations arose in the northern lands. By the turn of the next century, around 900, the fruits of these efforts would begin to show up. The fearsome Vikings would eventually be converted to Christianity and would take their place in Christian Europe. Anskar is justly remembered as the Apostle of the North.

Outline
by Chapter

The Formation of Christian Europe

Note to Readers: In this book, as explained in chapter one, we refer to regions of Europe by the modern names—such as Germany, France, and Italy—even though these countries did not exist in the years 600-900.

The *c.* before some dates is an abbreviation for *circa*, meaning "about" or "approximately."